Revolt!

Revolt! is a superb book, and Asimakopoulos knows that the crisis of the times demands nothing short of a complete transformation of capitalism into a socialist alternative. The time has come for a radical transformation of our social universe. The time has come for *Revolt!*

Dr. Peter McLaren
University of California, Los Angeles

Machine-breakers were once threatened with the death penalty if they took direct action against the systems of production that reduced them to poverty. Kleptocracy capitalism describes a similar juxtaposition: the facilitation of systematic corporate exploitation running alongside policies which criminalise individuals who steal in order to live. John Asimakopoulos' critique draws inspiration from the history of working-class activism and, in presenting a clear and accessible analysis of the system's operation, he also calls for direct action to combat it, passionately giving voice to a popular and deeply held view—that the status quo must be challenged.

Dr. Ruth Kinna,
Editor, *Anarchist Studies*

A welcome return to the center stage of political discourse—and action—for the working class, and class consciousness. A must read for everyone that actually takes working-class self-determination seriously.

Ramsey Kanaan,
PM Press

In our increasingly crisis-ridden world, where the global working class is rediscovering its spine, we need visions of vastly different worlds to aspire to. And these visions must be linked to critiques of the existing society. Asimakopoulos combines these tasks in his latest book, *Revolt!* This book is recommended reading for anyone sickened by an increasingly violent, volatile, and boring status quo.

Dr. Deric Shannon,
Transformative Radio

A must-read book for all those interested in real change and social justice stripped bare of rhetoric and fantasy.

Sarat Colling,
Political Media Review

The times are ripe for books like *Revolt!* Where the owning class has nearly succeeded in robbing the world blind in the most recent "global recession," works like *Revolt!* are crucial for forming effective class consciousness and resistance to political-economic tyranny. *Revolt!* is a healthy return to informed working class aggression, rather than the limp-spined liberalism that defines the "left" in US political discourse.

Dr. William Armaline,
Assistant Professor and Undergraduate Coordinator
Department of Justice Studies
San Jose State University

Revolt!

The Next Great Transformation from Kleptocracy Capitalism to Libertarian Socialism through Counter Ideology, Societal Education, & Direct Action

Dr. John Asimakopoulos

Transformative Studies Institute Press

Copyright © 2011 by John Asimakopoulos

Ideas in this book may be freely disseminated. Any properly attributed section or part of a chapter within the "fair use" guidelines may be used without permission. Any non-commercial educational use of this book or any part of it is granted permission. For all other uses please contact the Transformative Studies Institute for permissions.

An earlier version of Chapter 1 originally appeared in *Critical Sociology* 35, no. 2, 2009: 175–198.

Portions of Chapter 3 originally appeared in the *Journal of Poverty* 11, no. 2, 2007: 1–22.

Transformative Studies Institute Press
39-09 Berdan Avenue
Fair Lawn, NJ 07410 USA.

Publisher's Cataloging-in-Publication

Asimakopoulos, John.
Revolt! : the next great transformation from kleptocracy capitalism to libertarian socialism through counter ideology, societal education, & direct action / John Asimakopoulos. 1st ed. — Fair Lawn, NJ : Transformative Studies Institute Press, c2011.
  p. cm.
Includes bibliographical references and index.
ISBN: 978-0-9832982-0-5
  1. Globalization—Economic aspects. 2. Working class—United States. 3. Marxian economics. 4. Anarchism. 5. Social structure—United States. 6. Labor movement—United States. 7. Elite (Social sciences)—United States. 8. Civil rights movements—United States—History—20th century. 9. Critical pedagogy—United States. 10. Direct action. I. Transformative Studies Institute. II. Title.
HF1365 .A85 2011
337—dc22   2011921095

Royalties from this book will be donated to the endowment for the Transformative Studies Institute Graduate School—a free, accredited graduate school for the critical education of the working class.

Indexer, Proofreader: Chris Dodge
Cover Design: Kyung Ja Shin
Print Compilation: Sviatoslav Voloshin

For my parents George and Georgia

and

the workers of the world

Contents

Foreword, by Peter McLaren	i
Acknowledgments	xxiii
List of Tables and Figures	xxiv
Introduction	1
1 Kleptocracy Capitalism: Why Humpty Dumpty Must Always Fall	7
2 Counter Ideology: Radical Evolutionary Change	38
3 Societal Education: The Violent Labor Movement & The Civil Rights *Rebellion*	73
4 Direct Action: Loot the Rich	108
Conclusion: A Call to *Action!*	130
Bibliography	132
Index	143
About TSI	158
About the Author	159

Foreword

Tragedy is the representative trope—the leitmotif or idée force—of our age because its structural categories constitutively coincide with today's economic reality. And we know that this reality overlaps with itself, manufacturing a concomitant subjective awareness that regards itself as unsponsored and free—as forged by democracy. But we know that such a characterization is decidedly untrue. What distinguishes our democracy is that it is founded on affirming what its people decline to see, and this is made possible by a motivated amnesia, a thicket of confusion that keeps us from recognizing that our rights and livelihood are founded on violence, on a perpetual war waged by the propertied class against the poor. The selling of labor power for a wage (that includes most of us) to the capitalist class and the reality of racialized violence has, through the ages, haunted so-called democracies such as ours. People of color have viewed wage slavery and the vile persistence of racism as fellow travelers, as a dual nemesis, as two sides of the same coin known as neoliberal capitalism. In this era where past, present and future seem rolled into one, crashing into our brains like shrapnel, we lurch forward in a daze, finding it difficult to make sense of the depth and ubiquity of human depravity. We find meaningfulness in a life lived in the rearview mirror, ensuring that meaning is always retroactive, never immediate. There is never a transvaluation of time. All of life's fleeting shapes grow smaller. It brings us comfort because they are always behind us, and they can't affect us. We can't even recall how they got there.

I regret to inform my liberal friends and colleagues that we have moved well beyond the return of a progressive Keynesianism. That the domination of post-WWII economics by Fordism/Keynesianism is over (as the production of profit no longer relies upon the production of commodities and their sale) should not be a revelation to the most astute observers of the contemporary politics scene who have been examining in minute detail the collapse of our capitalist universe. Their most grim prognosis tells us that we have nowhere to run and nowhere to hide. What Pierre Bourdieu characterized in 1998 as a restoration of cynical capitalism by a conservative sociodicy—most notably, "the destruction of the economic and social bases of the most precious cultural gains of humanity" (1998, p. 37)—is an apposite description for capital's contemporary assault on everyday life.

We have arrived at a precipitous historical moment when either we slay the beast of capital, or it will slay us. Yes, we have reached the precipice of this stark choice. Because we can't see the profits of speculative capital as clearly as we can see the rising levels of state and federal debt or feel the strain of government cutbacks, the capitalist class has recognized a golden opportunity for some major ideological mystification by convincing the aggrieved working and middle classes that the reason for their unraveling living conditions is that the government is spending too much of their own money. By convincing voters to agree to government spending cuts on the grounds that debt levels threaten their standard of living, and by advising voters to put their faith in the machinations of white billionaires, the capitalist class is able to redistribute value from labor to capital without revealing how the whole corrupt system works. Then the climate is set for finding scapegoats for the current Great Recession and unleashing our embedded hatred for dark-skinned interlopers.

Oligarchies such as the US power elite benefit from the consolidation of numerous matrices of power, whose generation of surplus value potential is transnational in reach, and whose multifarious and decentralized institutional arrangements are organized around the industrial, bureaucratic and commodity models that have commonly been associated with the military industrial complex. All of these "power complexes" have intersecting social, cultural and political spheres that can be managed ideologically by means of powerful, all-encompassing corporate media apparatuses and the culture industry in general, including both popular and more traditional forms of religious dogma and practice.

We inhabit a social and economic system that is structured in terms of those who control the means of production and extract surplus labor from those who work for them. This is a society where social justice is reflected in an ethics of the ruling class who are determined at all costs to maintain social cohesion and economic prosperity and who seek the best conditions for its continuity. We know now that the financial crisis created the Great Recession, which then resulted in the fiscal crisis. Massive layoffs and unemployment followed the financial crisis. Peter Hudis (2010) is correct in stating that as inflated profits on fictitious capital dry up after the implosion of a speculative bubble, and capitalism must reduce the amount of variable capital relative to constant capital in order to restore profitability. Costs associated with providing public services go up as workers get laid off and tax revenues decline. The government uses taxpayer dollars to bail out the financial institutions that helped to create the financial crisis while those workers suffering most from the crisis are told that they are consuming too much and must be punished even further through austerity programs. The relative amount of value that goes to workers must be cut so that the succulent capitalist class can once again regain its appetite for the profits of speculative capital. Voters are told that debt levels threaten their economic well-being so out of fear they agree to cutbacks in government spending and this is how capital manages to redistribute value from labor to capital—forcing the poor to pay for the rising debt levels afflicting global capital.

Demanding that the rich and financial institutions pay for the crisis is not the answer, either, because, as Hudis (2010) notes, the relative proportion of value going to capital as against labor must be increased to guarantee that capital accumulation is sustained, and this is true even though 80% of the economic growth in the United States over the past 20 years has ended up in the hands of the wealthiest 5% of the population. Hudis (2010) warns us not to be misled by conceiving of social wealth as reducible to the revenue paid out to workers on the one hand and capitalists on the other. This is because most of the value produced in capitalism is not consumed by the capitalists or the workers, but by capital itself. When the Left demands that wealth be distributed to the poor this only intensifies the crisis of capital, so long as the capitalist law of value is not challenged. We know, for instance, that stagnation results when either capital or labor dominates the other. In free market periods capital dominates labor, leading to contraction caused by underconsumption and when labor dominates capital it leads to contraction due to a profit squeeze. Even if labor prevails through prolabor government policies, there would still be no lasting solution since a period in which labor is dominant would result in a profit squeeze which would trigger a recession (Asimakopoulos, *Revolt!*). We don't need to call for a redistribution of the wealth within capital's current value form. We need to uproot the very law of value itself. But in order to do that, we must create a viable conception of social organization that can replace capitalist value production. The Left has failed to do this and it is up to us now to take up the challenge.

Corporations now exert control over governments and the principles of global trade and financial regimes have segmented the world's workers into two regimes: the democratic West (or global North) based on consumption, with high wages and living standards, and the opposite who live in often nondemocratic nations based on authoritarian production, with low wages and living standards (Asimakopoulos, *Revolt!*). Having become absorbed into the very ideological fabric of the capitalist system and used as a vehicle for oppressing the more militant workers who take the struggle against oppression seriously, the labor movement itself has,

Foreword

in the United States at least, become a "cartel" rather than a hammer to break the chains of exploitation. Why don't workers reject the exploitative relations of production-consumption under capitalism in favor of autonomy and egalitarianism? The simplest answer is that we need to erode the legitimacy of the dominant ideology much further than do Rachel Maddox or John Stewart (bless them both) and create community control over corporate boards that involves codetermination rights, independent worker and community governance of the media and education that that could help the public learn about direct action, participatory democracy, and direct democracy. We need a democracy that can expand the functional dimension of public power from the traditional judiciary, legislative and executive powers to the people themselves. I would call this revolutionary democracy. Revolutionary democracy combines direct democracy and participatory democracy. Participatory democracy emphasizes the social, political, economic and cultural aspects of protagonist agency based on established discourses of human rights. Direct democracy refers to popular control of the means of production and organization by workers councils. Given that there appear to be no available means to convince those who control our economic system to adapt to changing economic conditions according to social needs instead of profits benefiting the corporations, the struggle for revolutionary democracy has become paramount. A precondition for socialism is the ideological development of a feasible alternative to existing hegemonic forms of social organization based on self-organization in civil society and self-direction in production (Asimakopoulos, *Revolt!*). That has yet to occur and we have little time left.

How the poor have endured for so long the cosmic arrogance of statutory poverty, racism, sexism and homophobia in the United States is any one's guess. The challenge today is to successfully stage manage the rage of downwardly mobile white folks whose social base is drawn from those formerly privileged sectors of the white working class that have been victims of the economic crisis, the deregulation of labor and global capital flight. This will not be easy since the right has opportunistically commandeered Christianity to bolster its quest for political power and to legitimize its interpretation of the current economic crisis. And the Southern Strategy that is part and parcel of the Tea Party Movement is moving us ever closer to a New Confederacy based on a re-feudalization of the economy and the creation of a new Jim Crow racial caste system by means of the imprisonment of people of color camouflaged by the argument that we live in a new post-racial society. With more African Americans under correctional control today than were enslaved in 1850, we are witnessing a new generation of African Americans living in the American Gulag who will lose their voting rights permanently as well as be denied employment, housing and a decent education as a result of the new engine of social policy toward African Americans—mass incarceration.

Historically, the United States has built its political theater on the schematic plan of a slave ship while the Gordian weave of the storyline has been masterminded by a playwright dressed in Boss Hogg's white flannel suit and slouched in a rocker on a rickety porch somewhere in the deep South. The tattered seam in the historical narrative of America that is most visible today is the unfinished business of Manifest Destiny and the treatment of formerly conquered peoples we call "illegals." But any successful dramatist knows that you can't treat undocumented immigrants like you could treat African Americans in the good old bullwhip days. And you can't forcefully annex half of Mexico like you could in the 1800s. So today you don't see Latina/os treed by packs of frenzied hounds, or rolled down ravines in barrels that have nails driven through them, or whipped for amusement, or lynched by jeering crowds—at least not on a regular basis. We've found new ways to rechannel repression and racism and unleash pent-up white anger and repudiation that extend beyond the increasingly militarized, 3000-kilometer US-Mexico border, where thousands of immigrants have died trying to cross "la linea."

In 1513 the conquistadores would read to the indigenous peoples of Las Americas a declaration of sovereignty and war, in the form of the *"Requerimiento,"* to assert their domination over the entire continent. This document maintained that through St. Peter and his papal successors God ruled the entire earth and that Pope Alexander VI conferred title over all the Americas to the Spanish monarchs. Those indigenous peoples who did not convert to Catholicism were to be made slaves and disposed of in any manner deemed appropriate by the Spanish. And if they refused, the *Requerimiento* stipulated that it was to be *their own fault.*

So instead of the *Requerimiento* being read threateningly from a brigantine anchored off the Yucatan peninsula to indigenous populations crowding the shoreline, we have gaining traction today paramilitary organizations such as the Minutemen, who volunteer to secure the border in T-shirts emblazoned with slogans such as "Kill a Mexican Today?" and who, with the backing of politicians, businessmen and wealthy ranchers, organize for-profit "human safaris" in the desert. While there, ordinary citizens can join the Minutemen in catching the "illegals" crossing the border, and if they are lucky, have an opportunity to indulge in

Foreword

some savage beatings (that is, if *la migra* isn't watching).

If this situation isn't disconcerting enough, there's the bill that stipulates the banning of ethnic studies in Arizona schools, HB 2281; and SB 1070, the racial profiling law; and SB 1097, the proposed law that will require children to identify the immigration status of their parents; and HB 2561/SB 1308 and HB 2562/SB1309—bills that seek to nullify birthright citizenship (guaranteed by the fourteenth amendment) to children whose parents cannot prove their legal status. But the most reactionary bill of all, recently introduced by state legislators is, SCR 1010, a bill that seeks to exempt Arizona from international laws. Copycat legislation from Arizona is springing up throughout the United States, as fifteen states have introduced legislation closely modeled on Arizona's law since the beginning of 2011. Legislators in other states are waiting for clarification from the courts before introducing similar measures. New legislation in the works is attacking the right of citizenship to so-called "anchor babies" or children born in the United States to migrant families (who might be stealth terrorists who would grow up hypnotically programmed to assassinate political figures).

Arizona wishes to preempt any opportunity to gain critical insight into the political workings of US society that might be offered in ethnic studies programs or that might compel the curious to question the status quo. Maintaining that ethnic studies programs teach hate, racial separation and the overthrow of the US government, the real target of HB 2281 is the Mexican American studies K–12 program in Tucson. It is dedicated to keeping Mexican American students from being able to write an essay like the one you are reading. The Mexican American studies K–12 program is not grounded in the revered Western canon, and its history does not commence with the pilgrim fathers; in contrast, the foundations of the program are built upon a 7,000-year-old maize-based curriculum in which students are taught indigenous (Mayan) concepts such as In Lak Ech (you are my other self), Panche Be (to seek the root of the truth) and Hunab Ku (we are all part of creation). This program has a 97.5% high school graduation rate. For the stentorian sentinels of public education, this amounts to sabotaging a rationally coordinated universe of multiple–choice tests with a pre-Cartesian unconsciousness and the disjointing of western monoculture and a curb on its relentless spread.

From the point of view of the oppressed, eliminating the course amounts to a form of cultural genocide, of epistemicide. What is the response by other states to this crisis of immigrant rights? As of this writing, fifteen more states want legislation modeled on Arizona's anti-immigration law (which is now on hold, pending court appeals).

Illustrative of the Right's distain for immigrant rights and the struggle for a more inclusive democracy is the popularity of Glenn Beck, the bloviating Mad Maestro, the Circus Clown of Broadcast Demagoguery, ranting and raving on the Republican Propaganda Machine (also known as Fox News/Fox Broadcasting Company). Beck is the Great Recession's Father Coughlin, the inflammatory Catholic priest broadcaster who galvanized millions of listeners into his shock troops each week against the twin evils of capitalism and communism. It's unfortunate that Father Coughlin called his 1934 organization the National Union for Social Justice, because his admiration for Hitler and Mussolini and his anti-Semitism has given social justice movements since that time a bad name. However, Beck is a palpably different from Coughlin. While morally repugnant, Coughlin was at least an intelligent fool. Beck is an unintelligent lunatic who believes Barack Obama is a Marxist and that social justice educators are hiding in every back alley off Main Street trying to bring down democracy. The Right is filled with shape shifters like Beck, who will hold any position that makes them look better to the emergent Tea Party movement. Take another well-known shape shifter, Mitt Romney. Romney's second book, *No Apology*, came out in 2010 in hardcover. In a revised paperback version, Romney changes his position on a number of issues. Not only does he pander to Glenn Beck and Joe the Plumber by mentioning them in the edition's new introduction, he cunningly shifts his position on the Recovery Act, from according it faint praise in the hardcover edition to pronouncing it a "failure" in the paperback edition. And apparently he now despises the Affordable Care Act, which resembled his own state-based health care law (Bernstein, 2011).

While the quisling Romney tries to figure out other ways to ingratiate himself with the Tea Party, I imagine Glenn Beck is already busy at work creating a new immigrant conspiracy, huddling around his chalkboard, chanting incantations from the *Clavicula Salomonis* or the Grimoire of Armadel like a deranged sorcerer's apprentice in Imperial Wizard regalia, trying to summon the ghost of The Gipper to help him launch a Contra-like war on undocumented Mexicans. And, of course, link it all in his blog, *Blaze*, to Acorn, SDS, George Soros, the Open Society Institute, the Cloward-Piven Plan (hatched in the *Nation* magazine in 1966), or to a secret Egyptian caliphate hidden in the bowels of the Great Pyramid of Giza and personally administered by Barack Obama.

The election of a black president and fear of the increasing racial diversity of the population—fear that the country could become a majority of "dark skinned races"—has enraged disenfranchised white workers and the diminishing middle class. On the home front, the curtain was drawn

Foreword

back on the Potemkin village we call America by Jared Loughner's attempted assassination of Rep. Gabrielle Giffords in Tucson. The far right urges vigilante tactics while condemning violence, quite the feat of political legerdemain. But what no one is attempting to hide is the racism spawning in the fetid arteries of those who are panicking at the impending disappearance of the Great White Nation. The spectacle of the attack on Giffords shed light on the routine vigilantism directed daily at migrants and people of color.

But what is happening at the level of Arizona is writ large internationally in the malignant form of US foreign policy. The faux reality surrounding President Hugo Chavez (a harsh critic of US imperialism) has been craftily created by the "perception managers" of the US media, as Chavez is often referred to as a "dictator," whereas Egypt's murderous Mubarek (largely a puppet of the United States) was referred to as "president" (fortunately now defunct). Recently, critics of the Venezuelan "dictator" from the "counterrevolutionaries" (I hate to use the term "opposition") have accused him of remaking Venezuela's higher education system into a massive propaganda machine (something akin to a leftist Fox News). These are critics who obviously don't trust the notion of social equity through popular action. It appears that they are at a loss to know how to respond to an education system in which respect is accorded learning, embedded within an ecology of knowledge as opposed to a monoculture of knowledge, in which the goal of education is not to produce human capital but a critical citizenry, and not to create an entrepreneurial-competitive global elite but social justice on a global scale.

When education is designed to serve the entire society and is not narrowly conceived as the enhancement of social mobility within the larger capitalist social order, it cannot be articulated only or mainly in positivistic quantifiable standards. Granted, the 2,000 newly created *aldeas universitarias* housed in educational institutions, prisons, military garrisons, and libraries throughout all of the 335 municipalities in Venezuela might not count much in terms of international standards of academic prestige. When a central criterion of successful education rests upon the notion of improving the living conditions of the Venezuelan people, this might not help Venezuela's universities compete in the top 1,000 of world academic institutions, but it is a standard that world-class universities would do well to follow. If we regard the Cuban literacy campaign as the greatest educational achievement of the past 100 years, then Chavez's achievement of an illiteracy-free Venezuela would surely count as a runner-up. But do these standards matter to the critics of the revolution? While I am sure Chavez's critics would not like to return to the days of the late

Fourth Republic when universities and colleges were places that allocated according to socio-geographical criteria such as place of residence (in which case applicants from *los barrios pobres* would be automatically excluded,) or when the law faculties would demand strict dress codes (which would exclude from studying law those who could not afford the right clothes), it is clear that they find the goal of socialism for the twenty-first century a hard pill to swallow. Clearly, by advancing the economic, social, and cultural role of education as a part of local, national and regional endogenous development for the purpose of creating a twenty-first century socialism dedicated to both participatory and direct democracy, Venezuela is undertaking an ethical and moral re-foundation of the nation. Moving toward economic equality requires not only long-term structural transformation but a rescaling of power from the bourgeoisie and private managerial elite to those toiling in the barrios. Contrast Chavez's Bolivarian initiative with a recent state appeals court ruling in New York that the state was obliged to provide no more than a middle-school-level education, and to prepare students for nothing more than the lowest-level jobs (Perez-Pena, 2002). Contrast developments in Venezuela with the partnering of neoliberal education initiatives with social conservatives in the for-profit charter school movement in the United States. Contrast Venezuela to the NEA and the AFT teachers' unions in the United States, who overwhelmingly accept neoliberalism's definition of democracy and view the world of learning and knowledge production through the eyes of US capitalism.

Recently Hillary Clinton rushed off to Haiti, alarmed that this tiny and impoverished country was demanding free elections. Apparently the Haitian government had the temerity to refuse to reverse the results of the first round of its November 2010 presidential elections, much to the chagrin of the United States who supports (no surprise here) the right-wing candidate. So the US threatened to cut aid to Haiti if Jude Celestin was not knocked down from first to third place. Furthermore, the US had made sure that Haiti's most popular political party, Fanmi Lavalas, which supports former president Jean-Bertrand Aristide, was banned from participating in the November elections. The US is furious that the Haitian government has decided to issue a diplomatic passport to Aristide, who has been in exile in South Africa since he was ousted by a US-organized coup. Not only did the US organize the 2004 coup, but they have given support to the anti-Aristide death squads since 1991. But, of course, this is just business as usual. After all, the United States is not your garden variety imperialist nation.

The news media are sick with celebrations of the centennial of the birth of Ronald Reagan, who spent many of those storied years under klieg lights before he moved into the White House. At the same time they are relatively silent about the cancellation of a speech in Switzerland by George W. Bush due to a fear he might end up, like the late Augusto Pinochet, arrested outside his country for his war crimes—in Bush's case for his torture of prisoners at Guantánamo Bay.

Republicans hold unfaltering that Reagan, the Great Communicator, was one of the greatest of all US presidents and assume unshakably that he was morally untainted. I hate to spoil the party but Reagan ran a criminal administration that, by the end of his term, witnessed 138 administration officials convicted, indicted, or the subject of official investigations for official misconduct and/or criminal violations. How could we forget the gap-toothed and straight-backed Oliver North, who was indicted on sixteen felony counts and on May 4, 1989, was convicted of three: accepting an illegal gratuity, aiding and abetting in the obstruction of a congressional inquiry, and destruction of documents. He was sentenced on July 5, 1989, to a three-year suspended prison term, two years probation, $150,000 in fines, and 1,200 hours of community service. His conviction would later be overturned. The Reagan Gang covered up many atrocities in Latin America and elsewhere. He might have been America's friendly grandfather, always ready with a bowl of jelly beans to accompany his superficial geniality, but what did he actually do with his power?

The myth that Reagan "won the Cold War"—even though his belligerent attitude toward the Soviet Union may have actually extended the Cold War—has diverted retrospective attention from the tyranny of his foreign policy built upon Manifest Destiny, socially reactionary theocratic ideology, and his war on America's poor (and especially people of color). Reagan widened the income gap between the rich and the poor, eroded the standard of living of millions of low-wage workers, and dramatically increased the number of people living beneath the federal poverty line.

Reagan's infamous attack on striking air traffic controllers early in his presidency is compared to Margaret Thatcher's crushing of the miner's strike in England in terms of advancing the cause of neoliberal capitalism and leaving the welfare state in ruins. In fact, Reagan made union bashing a popular pastime among Americans, when they were not exploiting white male resentment by denouncing the African-American "welfare queens" so brutally demonized by Reagan (the example of the Chicago "welfare queen" described by Reagan as driving a Cadillac, cheating the government out of $150,000 by using eighty aliases, thirty addresses, a dozen Social Security cards and four fictional dead husbands, was later proven to be fictitious). The economic prosperity that Reagan brought to the nation benefited the rich, not the poor, and the savings and loan scandal under his presidential watch offered a prophetic glimpse of the frenzied action on futures-trading floors at the dawn of the credit crisis, and intimated what might be in store for future Americans if the banks were allowed to go berserk (something gleefully facilitated by Reagan's fiscal policies of deregulation).

Reagan's avuncular persona often camouflaged his unflinching support of right-wing death squads in Central and South America. His chilling aid to regimes engaged in genocide should have had Reagan denounced by the American public as a heinous ideologue and war criminal. But, of course, the hundreds of thousands of the victims of the "dirty wars" he supported were leftists, so this gave cause for Americans to rationalize Reagan's complicity in murder and torture on a mass scale.

As a columnist during the Carter administration Reagan would defend the murderous Argentine junta. When Reagan was elected president in November 1980, he directed the CIA to work with the Argentine intelligence service training and arming the Nicaraguan Contras, a group of thugs who carried out atrocities against the Sandanistas, attacking purely civilian targets utilizing tactics that included murder, rape, beatings, kidnapping and disruption of harvests (including the torture and murder of women and children). The Contras were aided by an "assassination manual" prepared by the CIA specifically for their use. Reagan also supported the right-wing Salvadorean military, and the "dirty war" in Guatemala. By lifting the ban on military aid to Guatemala and sending military equipment to the Guatemalan military to aid them in counterinsurgency and paramilitary operations, Reagan was guilty of aiding and abetting acts of government-sponsored genocide against leftist rebels and their sympathizers. Reagan proclaimed the notorious Guatemalan general Efrain Rios Montt to be "a man of great personal integrity" even as Rios Montt began a murderous campaign that utilized seasoned death squads to kidnap, torture and murder students and teachers and union members and carry out a bloody campaign against the indigenous population suspected of supporting guerrilla insurgents, and in the process wiping out entire Mayan villages in the northern highlands. Reports during those years described children thrown into burning homes by the "Archivo" hit squads or tossed like rag dolls into the air and impaled upon bayonets. And then there was the imfamous Ratealhuleu death camp which the Guatemalan military failed to cover up, a situation that makes Abu Graib look tame in comparison.

Foreword

Despite Reagan's monstrous foreign policy legacy, including his administration's arming and training of native mujahedeen "freedom fighters" from Afghanistan, whom he likened to America's founding fathers—some of whom went on to form the Taliban—during the 1990s he was being manufactured by the corporate media and its Republican backers as an impervious and unassailable national icon. In the spirit of Reagan's sordid legacy, Wisconsin's new Republican governor, Scott Walker, has recently succeeded in taking away the bargaining rights of nearly all government workers and in the process he warned reporters that he had alerted the National Guard in case there was an interruption of state services or heated reaction from the workers. While law enforcement and fire fighting employees as well as state troopers and inspectors are exempt from the law, all other state workers are prohibited from negotiating for better pensions and health benefits. Walker's role in the demise of democracy in Wisconsin would be risible if it were not so tragic.

If the struggle for democracy is in retreat in the United States, it is certainly on the rise in the Middle East. In Egypt, Iraq, Tunisia, Lebanon, and elsewhere, we are witnessing the Arab world resisting US-backed tyranny and the diminished capacity of the United States to shape events. But they are up against a formidable enemy, one as powerful as the warships of the US Fifth Fleet traveling through the Suez Canal: state controlled and corporate media.

The media shape the contours of our subjective formation as they wrap us up in the pedagogy of the spectacle. In the United States, the state encourages various forms of desublimation and freedom in order to distract attention from the oppressive and authoritarian dimensions of capitalist society. People are too willing to give over their sovereignty and liberty to tyrants—even gleefully willing!—in favor of imbibing the sensuality of the media spectacle and the drab but familiar commodification of everyday life in *las entranas de la bestia*. This has transmogrified into a renewed growth of the racist right wing, accompanied by a populist, reactionary agenda.

Recently in Morelia, Michoacán, at the *Volver a Marx* conference, I joined thousands of workers and teachers gathered together to listen to Mexican and international speakers talk about social change.

Volver a Marx brought together a cross section of the working class of Mexico and Latin America—teachers, students, peasants, intellectuals, artists, and unemployed workers—to commit themselves to fighting the forces of imperialism and its allies, to protest the national oligarchy's war against the people, and to design their own strategies for resistance from an analysis of the current situation.

I was apprehensive about going to Morelia, given the activity of La Familia Michoacana, which formed in the 1980s with the stated purpose of bringing order to Michoacán, emphasizing help and protection for the poor. It originally began as a vigilante group organized to respond to trespassing kidnappers and drug dealers, who were their acknowledged enemies. However, La Familia eventually transitioned into a powerful and ruthless criminal gang, more specifically as a paramilitary gang of the Gulf Cartel who trained with Los Zetas and then formed themselves into an independent drug trafficking operation. La Familia is now a major rival to Los Zetas and the Beltrán-Leyva Cartel, but maintains a strategic alliance with the Sinaloa Cartel of "El Chapo" Guzmán (Joaquín Archivaldo Guzmán Loera).

La Familia Michoacana has been referred to as a quasi-religious cult that mixes an evangelical-style self-help philosophy with slogans from the Mexican Revolution. Not only does La Familia cartel emphasize religion and family values, it gives loans to farmers, businesses, schools and churches, and claims in newspaper advertisements that it does not tolerate substance abuse or exploitation of women and children. La Familia's assassinations and beheadings are often referred to by members as a form of "divine justice" and it appears likely that they have some ties with devotees of Swedenborgianism, or the Church of the New Jerusalem religious movement, which promotes a social justice agenda. While I was in Michoacán, La Familia's spiritual leader, El Más Loco (Nazario Moreno González), who was raised a Catholic but became a Jehovah's Witness, was gunned down in Apatzingán, the hot Tierra Caliente valley, in the west-central part of Michoacán, during a battle with federal police. During the shootout, in an attempt to prevent reinforcements from arriving from Morelia, they surrounded the city, using burning vehicles as barricades. El Más Loco appears to have been influenced by the "open theism" movement, and especially the work of Christian writer John Eldredge. Open theism advocates a personal God who can be influenced by prayer and the actions of people. Before launching his own Ransomed Heart Ministries, Eldredge worked with James Dobson's evangelical megachurch movement, Focus on the Family, in Colorado Springs, an influential right-wing organization that promotes Christian family counselling as well as a socially conservative public policy. In his bestselling book, *Wild at Heart* (not to be confused with David Lynch's film, based on Barry Gifford's novel of the same title), Eldredge criticizes Christian men for refusing to pay attention to their deepest desires. El Más Loco of La Familia had made Eldredge's book, translated into

Foreword

Spanish as *Salvaje de Corazón*, required reading for La Familia gang members and allegedly paid rural teachers and National Development Education members to circulate Eldredge's writings throughout the countryside of Michoacán. I knew La Familia was one of Mexico's fastest growing drug cartels, operated "superlabs," and had become Mexico's largest supplier of methamphetamines to the United States. I had also read that in Uruapan, in 2006, some cartel members tossed five decapitated heads onto the dance floor of the Sol y Sombra night club along with the chilling message: *"The Family doesn't kill for money. It doesn't kill women. It doesn't kill innocent people, only those who deserve to die. Know that this is divine justice."*

I wasn't sure where exactly critical pedagogy would fit with La Familia's social justice agenda, and wondered if any members or sympathizers of La Familia might be sitting in the audience taking notes. I began to think of how social justice as a political agenda can be misguided and corrupted by quasi-religious justifications for violence, and how charismatic leaders can provoke heinous acts in the name of creating a better future for the poor and the powerless. I began to think of what was happening in my adopted country of the United States, where some prominent Christian leaders were denouncing the separation of religion and the state and endorsing an all-out Holy War against Islam. These are the leaders who supported the war in Iraq and currently in Afghanistan on a religious basis, and whose constituents, who are daily consumers of Fox News, believe President Obama is really a Muslim using his office in a clandestine way to bring about the defeat of Christianity.

While automatic weapons firing throughout the night kept some of us sleepless, the conference continued, and as the fires in the passengers buses burned themselves out, the conference participants produced a document called Declaracion de Morelia, and we held a press conference and presented it to the local media. Afterward, I met with leaders of the Otomi, Nahuatl, P'urhepecha and Nhanu groups, and was invited to participate in the creation of thirty indigenous schools.

The Declaration of Morelia reaffirmed the conviction of the participants that Marxism is a living and humanistic theory, not a militant dogma, essential not only to understand the complexity of today's capitalist world, but to provide the theoretical tools to transform it. During one of the sessions devoted to drafting the document, in which critical pedagogy was discussed as a model for education in Michoacán, several workers asked that WikiLeaks be mentioned for its important role in speaking truth to power. And I couldn't help but recall the demand from some US administration officials that Julian Assange, the founder of Wikileaks, be executed. WikiLeaks is a form of activist journalism that we need to cultivate today. In a talk I gave years ago with Daniel Ellsberg, I remember how vehemently he decried the selling out of journalism to the dictates of the corporate media bosses. It made it seem all the more perversely hypocritical that on the very day that WikiLeaks posted US State Department cables showing that the Obama administration was aware of and complicit in Mubarak's use of torture and murder against his political opponents, President Obama criticized Mubarak about Egypt's human rights record. Meanwhile, criticism of Assange continues apace. Republican Rep. Peter King of New York called for Assange to be charged under the Espionage Act and asked whether WikiLeaks could be designated a terrorist organization. Tom Flanagan, a former aide to Canadian Prime Minister Stephen Harper, called for Assange's assassination, while Sarah Palin described Assange as an "anti-American operative with blood on his hands" in a Facebook message. Mike Huckabee, like Palin a potential Republican presidential candidate, also said the person who leaked the information to Assange should be tried for treason and executed.

It is not surprising that those who most benefit from keeping the public in the dark about the historical machinations of "democracies" such as ours would be the most vigorous voices calling for the death of those who dare to pull back the curtain of the wizard.

It has occurred to me that La Familia Michoacana is not that much different than the Cult of American Divine Violence. Americans accept violence as part of the providential history that their Christian God has bequeathed to them. The blood of its imperial victims is America's baptismal waters. Vietnam, Korea, Hiroshima and Nagasaki, the lands of the original indigenous populations of the United States: all of the violence exercised in these campaigns of bloodshed was blessed, sacred violence carried out as part of a civilizing mission to bring democracy to an uncivilized world.

Bill Blum writes:

> But war can be seen as America's religion — most recently Pakistan, Iraq, Afghanistan, Somalia, Yemen, and many more in the past — all non-believers in Washington's Church of Our Lady of Eternal Invasion, Sacred Bombing, and Immaculate Torture, all condemned to death for blasphemy, as each day the United States unleashes blessed robotic death machines called Predators flying over their lands to send "Hellfire" (sic) missiles screaming into wedding parties, funerals, homes, not knowing who the victims are, not caring who the victims are, thousands of them by now, as long as Wash-

Foreword

ington can claim each time—whether correctly or not—that amongst their number was a prominent blasphemer, call him Taliban, or al Qaeda, or insurgent, or militant. How can we reason with such people, the ones in the CIA who operate these drone bombers? What is the difference between them and Mumtaz Qadri? Qadri was smiling in satisfaction after carrying out his holy mission. The CIA man sits comfortably in a room in Nevada and plays his holy video game, then goes out to a satisfying dinner while his victims lay dying. Mumtaz Qadri believes passionately in something called Paradise. The CIA man believes passionately in something called American Exceptionalism. As do the great majority of Americans. Our drone operator is not necessarily an "extremist."

Our prophets are the arms dealers who worship at the altars of Lockheed Martin, General Dynamics, Boeing and Raytheon who produce all kinds of conventional weapons of death—and it is the conventional weapons such as tanks, drones, fighter jets and missiles, that are the real weapons of mass destruction, especially in the hands of Washington's oil-first "realists." Those who worship the profits of blood are not going to be inclined to listen to those who want to stop and repair the violence that our cult of violence has spawned.

Critical pedagogy teaches us that we have the collective power to overcome the inimical forces of capital. The promised land is not a glimpse of a lush dream, the sun shining on the window soffit. Nor is it only to be found in the verdant fields of the imagination. It is very much where we happen to be standing as we attempt to transform the world of capital into a world free of necessity. The promised land can therefore only promise to be a place of struggle, springing up in the dark, silent, underground crypts and caves where revolutionary futures incubate and where hope is conjugated with the movement of the people toward an anti-capitalist future. We are all merely seeds in the moist soil of the counter-world. It is up to us to decide what that world is to look like and how to get there.

We need to extend the ambit of critical pedagogy from persons with "authority" to whom by convention and precept education has hitherto largely been confined, to those who are "least" among us, not in numbers, surely, but in social legitimacy—the poor and the dispossessed. I am not talking about the dispossessed as dispossessed but as a revolutionary force for socialism. They are carrying a much larger freight than their single selves. It is in their name that we begin to unravel what we have been formed to be, and begin the arduous and painful process of remaking ourselves in a deliberately new way. The new way often takes us on a collision course with the systems of intelligibility, ways of knowing, and received terms that we have inherited.

The fact is, surely, that we are faced with two choices of life—the liberal model of pleading with corporations to temper their cruelty and greed, or the reactionary model that has declared war on social and economic equality. And on the evidence that each of these models are fiercely and hopelessly entangled in each other's conflictual embrace, we can accept neither.

Critical pedagogy is more than throaty bursts of teacherly impropriety, more than enumerating in ironic detail the problems faced by the youth of today, more than hurling invective at government policies, but a sustained march toward a revolutionary consciousness and praxis.

We must become more like the unknown sailor who tried to smash the statue of Napoleon's head with a brick during the days of the Paris Commune, or like the Iraqi journalist who threw his shoe at the head of President George W. Bush who, standing before the cameras of the transnational corporate media like a Texas version of the Vendome Column wrapped in a jock strap, became an hideous effigy that stood for the decomposition of civilization through the power of lies and military aggression.

Revolutionary critical pedagogy questions the official, hegemonic view of ahistorical educational change, isolated from the capitalist social and production relationships. As critical revolutionary educators, we need to understand how the dynamics of the capitalist system—its movement from global capitalism to transnational capital, for instance—has guided the meaning and purpose of educational reform and has impacted institutions and approaches with respect to what counts as educational change.

We follow Che's dialectical conception of education which is formed internally through analyzing the continuous contractions of external influences on the life of individuals. We agree with Paulo Freire that dialogical pedagogy can achieve the kind of class consciousness necessary for a powerful social transformation. This also suggests that as we participate in an analysis of the objective social totality, that we simultaneously struggle for a social universe outside of the value form of labor. If we are to educate at all, we must educate for this! Statist socialism has collapsed and weighs heavier on the minds of the living with its inevitable decay into the oblivion of historical time. Libertarian socialism as well lies rotting on its deathbed, as capitalism continues to wreak its revenge, despite its present state of unprecedented crisis. Antisystemic movements of all shapes and stripes are still around but have, for the most part, become domesticated into reformist shadows of their previous revolutionary selves, forming enfeebled and enfeebling popular fronts that fall like spent cartridges on the heels of any real challenge to capitalism. Here we need a pedagogy of revolt that can deepen the organization and development of popular fronts, so that educators can work within and against the state from a war of position in which self-interested individuals understand that they need the support of individuals, as in trade union consciousness, and move from here to developing solidarity with others who have a shared economic interest with them, to a realization that the interests of their oppressed groups need to be taken up by other oppressed groups as well—in other words, a move from trade union consciousness or a class-in-itself, to a class-for-itself. To come together as a class of individuals conscious of sharing a common social situation and who unite to pursue common interests requires a revolutionary critical pedagogy that is able to struggle against the existing capitalist hegemony which relies heavily on ideological consent-building, that is, on actively selling its vision to subordinate classes, a vision grounded in bourgeois economics. Here critical educators must take a stand, working for a political or direct democracy, for the direct control of the political process by citizens, for economic democracy, for the ownership and direct control of economic resources by the citizen body, for democracy in the social realm by means of self-management of educational institutions and workplaces, and for the ecological justice that will enable us to reintegrate society into nature. The struggle for a new historic bloc built up by the working class will not be easy. If critical educational studies is to avoid being corralled into accepting the dominant ideology, or annexed to pro-capitalist forces among the left, or transformed into a recruiting ground for liberal reform efforts, or even worse, turned into an outpost for reactionary populism, it will largely be due to the efforts of revolutionary critical educators.

We need to struggle for an autonomous society in which the public space encompasses the entire citizen body, and where we can exercise a direct democracy (what is also called inclusive democracy), where decisions at the macro level (i.e., economic and political decisions) are part of an institutional framework of equal distribution of political and economic power among citizens. Such a space requires a socialist alternative to capitalism. Here we have a different conception of freedom than the free marketeers: freedom to achieve self-determination and participate in society's reflective and deliberative activities to bring a substantive content to the public sphere. In that sense, we must deny capitalism as the ultimate social horizon. We have to organize a new push toward a post-capitalist future. We need to challenge repressive and violent social structures because the current world system has no intention of changing.

Our harvest of justice, yet to be garnered, will be forthcoming only when we are prepared to fight in the long haul, and this means working hard to emancipate ourselves from the thralldom of commonsense which, we have learned, is not really the applied wisdom of the common people, but the ideology of the capitalist class camouflaged as the burdensome collectivity of the popular majorities. Only then can we begin to rehabilitate the dignity of human life.

We need to awaken from our dream into another dream, but one dreamt with open eyes, a collective dream that will take us out of the homogeneous, monumental and chronological time of capital and beyond the consolatory pretensions of the bourgeoisie to create the "time of the now" discussed so poignantly by Benjamin—the time of the revolutionary. We need to capture the revolutionary fervor of the communards, whose battle-tested hearts managed, if only for a brief time, to pump into the sewers of history the muck of ages lining the drainpipes of a lost revolution. It is precisely the socialist partisanship of critical pedagogy—not to the point of dogmatism or inflexibility—that reveals its power of critique. We need to reclaim the power of critique as the sword arm of social justice and not relinquish it. For in doing so we reclaim our humanity and the world.

When the commissioner of the New York State Department of Education, David M. Steiner, warned Henry Giroux at the Nexus Conference in Amsterdam in 2007 that "social justice promotes hatred for the established order", it became clearer what the internal ideological compass was that guided the Right—that the object of attack of many establishment leaders in education, such as Steiner, is critical thought itself. Steiner's remarks are a prime example of heaping ideological mystification upon distortion. But the real pathos is not the mystification nor the distortion of the truth, it is the fact that critique itself is now seen as a major enemy of education. What we are facing are not only retrograde positivists who champion instrumental rationality, but also, as Giroux notes, conservative ideologues who promote authoritarian forms of pedagogy that are in direct conflict with the concept of an open, participatory democracy.

Critical pedagogy advocates self-education by accessing independent media, by learning how to identify and analyze social injustice. While the sedulousness of the left has never been in doubt, it needs to be accompanied by a detailed vision of what a social universe outside the value form of labor might look like. If we accomplish that task, then we can move from discussion of redistributing the wealth within the existing capitalist system to changing the system of value production itself.

It is becoming increasingly clear that teachers are not content playing the part of compliant ideological servants of structural injustice. Critical pedagogy creates spaces where the laws of estrangement do not dominate. Needed are pedagogies of the kind that are being banned in Arizona, and others that can deepen the organization and development of popular fronts, so that educators can work within and against the state from a war of position in which self-interested individuals understand that they need the support of individuals, as in trade union consciousness, and move from here to developing solidarity with others who have a shared economic interest with them, to a realization that the interests of their oppressed group needs to be taken up by other oppressed groups as well—in other words, a move from trade union consciousness and a class-in-itself, to revolutionary consciousness, and a class-for-itself. To come together as a class of individuals conscious of sharing a common social situation, to unite to pursue common interests, requires a revolutionary critical pedagogy that is able to struggle against the existing capitalist hegemony which relies heavily on ideological consent-building, that is, on actively selling its fraudulent vision to the subordinate classes. But how do we do this? First, we can begin to conceive of critical pedagogy as a social movement, actively promoting what Henry Giroux calls public pedagogy, as a means of democratizing the public sphere and creating forms of transnational activism and Social Movement Unionism. We should definitely learn from the labor movement of the past, from the literature and theater of the 1920s and 1930s that shed public light on the struggles of working families. For the past twenty years, I have been showing my students a National Endowment for the Humanities film by Suzanne Bauman and Rita Heller called *Women of Summer*. The film captures a prodigious moment in our history when unionists, educators and feminists joined in a collective project from 1921 to 1938. It was during this time that 1,700 blue collar women participated in a great educational experiment known as the Bryn Mawr Summer School of Women Workers. Here was labor education at its best. Utilizing both leftist principles and theories and a progressive educational philosophy indebted to the work of John Dewey, the teachers at Bryn Mawr believed that workers' education should reflect workers' practical experience in the production process, as a way of developing a pedagogical approach that would lead to transformative social change. We could, for instance, bring back labor colleges and groups modeled on the examples of Brookwood and the Worker Education Bureau. And we should develop more organizations like the still-surviving Highlander Folk School. But most of all we need a feasible alternative to existing forms of societal organization that reproduce labor's value form. And that will require educators, economists, philosophers, rural and urban planners, critical geographers, anthropologists and sociologists, technology specialists, communication experts, social theorists and social activists coming together with community workers and representatives to work jointly on a solution. And where is one of the best places to find all of these specialists in one place—the university. However, the increasing privatization and corporatization of higher education is more likely to lead to a resocialization of the perceptions of the population into the dominant legitimizing myths of capitalism than to finding an alternative to value production.

The American Mind, even in its death rattle, has an unacceptably cavalier attitude to the living conditions of the poor and the ebb and flow of their daily lives. There is no repentance in the work for those holding such an attitude. The American Mind is a stubborn Methuselah. Should we abandon the American Mind in its final imperial moments? Or is there still something worthwhile to learn from the revolutionary aspects of its consciousness that are still repressed, but in deep retreat, far inside?

These are questions that can inspire workers, scholars, college students and activists to engage John Asimakopoulos' powerful tome, *Revolt!*. In this urgent work, Asimakopoulos' incisive analysis of the current crisis of capitalism and prescient challenge to the brutal advance of neoliberal globalization serve as a clarion call to those who yearn for social justice and are willing to undertake direct action for evolutionary radical change, beginning with an immediate challenge to capitalism. For Asimakopoulos, direct action, societal education, and libertarian socialism is an inseparable combination needed to bring real results to the struggle for our emancipation from necessity. His proposals deserve serious consideration: the use of direct action to demand that all corporate boards of directors be comprised exclusively by worker and community representatives; the nationalization of all educational institutions and free education at all levels; universal free housing; guaranteed food, utilities and services; single-payer, free health care—issues that in the United States would never be permitted a serious voice in the corporate-controlled media let alone sanctioned by any legislative body.

Revolt! distinguishes itself for its repeated insistence on the critical production of knowledge and not its petrified systematizing, its faith in the direct action of people in struggle for a better life for themselves and their communities and not faith in an ideology, a leader, or program, because the latter leads us not to wisdom but to a proclamation of finalities. *Revolt!* is about epochal change. It is about taking action to change the world.

Revolt! is a superb book, and Asimakopoulos knows that the crisis of the times demands nothing short of a complete transformation of capitalism into a socialist alternative. The time has come for a radical transformation of our social universe. The time has come for *Revolt*!

Peter McLaren
University of California, Los Angeles

Notes

This foreword is an expanded version of Peter McLaren, "The Death Rattle of the American Mind", *Cultural Studies/Critical Methodologies*, forthcoming, and also Peter McLaren, "Revolutionary Critical Pedagogy for a Socialist Society: A Manifesto", *Capilano Review* 3, no. 13 (Winter, 2011), 61–66.

References

Bernstein, David. (2011). "Mitt Rewrites Himself". *Boston Phoenix*, February 11.
Blum, Bill. (2011). *The Anti-Empire Report*. February 3, http://killinghope.org/bblum6/aer90.html.
Bourdieu, Pierre. (1998). *Acts of Resistance: Against the Tyranny of the Market*. New York: New Press.
Declaration de Morelia, http://www.fundacionmclaren.com/
Hudis, Peter. (2010). "Dialectics of Economic Turbulence". U.S. Marxist-Humanists. December 15. http://www.usmarxisthumanists.org/
Perez-Pena, R. (2002). "Court Reverses Finance Ruling on City Schools". *New York Times*, June 26, A1.

Acknowledgments

I am deeply grateful to my old friend and colleague Dr. Ali Zaidi for his friendship and countless agonizing hours of editing. I also thank my friends, colleagues, and family for their support throughout the years. Special thanks to my mother and father Georgia and George, Elsa Karen Márquez-Aponte, Sviatoslav (Svet) Voloshin, and Kyung Ja (Sindy) Shin. Special gratitude is owed to Dr. Peter McLaren, a pillar of critical pedagogy, for his contribution and support.

All ideas and opinions in this book are exclusively the author's.

This work was supported (in part) by Grants #62063-00 40 and #68131-00 37 from the City University of New York PSC-CUNY Research Award Program; the Faculty Fellowship Publication Program-CUNY; and the National University of Ireland, Galway.

List of Tables and Figures

Tables:

Table 1. Total Number of
Regional Trade Agreements 1948–2002 15

Table 2. Average Yearly Percent Growth of
Real GDP per Capita (using PPP in 2005 dollars) 22

Table 3. Growth Rates of Disposable Personal Income,
Consumption, and Saving, 2000–2005 24

Table 4. Power, Contraction, and Expansion 46

Table 5. Wealth Distribution in 2001 59

Table 6. Strike Activity 1883–1886 83

Table 7. Race Revolts 1917–1977 91

Table 8. Key Events of the Civil Rights Movement 92

Figures:

Figure 1. The Global Production-Consumption Model 19

Figure 2. The Corporate Control Model 41

Figure 3. Total Societal Wealth 49

Figure 4. Dialectical Change and Libertarian Socialism 51

Introduction

"Political rights do not originate in parliaments."

Rudolf Rocker

Although they often profess sympathy for the poor and exploited, professors, like other professionals, actually do very little on their behalf. The solutions that they propose tend to be ineffectual if not disingenuous. Go vote, they advise, without considering what that means to a black who is disenfranchised because of a felony conviction, or what it means to a voter faced with two electoral choices between which there is little to differentiate. These illusory solutions fail because professors generally do not know what it takes to bring about change, and are reluctant to challenge a system that tosses them a few crumbs from the banquet of privilege—such as summer vacation—and which destroys careers in reprisal.[1] Worse, many are simply petit bourgeois (middle class) and have no intention to fundamentally challenge the master.

Those are some of the same so-called "educators" who told me my introduction to this book claims it is simple to understand for the everyday worker. But the actual body of it is academic and sophisticated. At first, this was worrisome given my intention to do for workers of the world what I do every day for my working-class students in the Bronx: make sense of what seems complicated. And then I thought of Georgia, my mother. At age seventy-three with a third-grade education, this woman who grew up blind in one eye, worked on farms and in factories never doing any intellectual activity, sat and read all three volumes of Marx's *Capital* cover to cover, notes and all as I was writing this book. When I asked "how much did you understand?" she replied, "everything—I have experienced what he writes about." So, for me, a worker is always capable of understanding it just may take a bit more effort.

As the son of Greek landless farmers, I witnessed injustice and exploitation from an early age. Later, as a working-class student in the United States, I could not attend the graduate schools of my choice because of the structural inequities of higher education. And as a professor I experienced academic repression first hand when I was, in the words of the labor arbitrator who reinstated me, "arbitrarily and capriciously fired"[2]. There was, however, nothing arbitrary or capricious about my firing: I had stood up for my rights and those of my students. More so, I was publishing works on anarchism and Marxism. Censorship is alive and well in this nation of illusionary freedoms.

Finally I decided that enough was enough. The time had come for an "organic intellectual" such as myself, to quote Gramsci, to tell it like it is. Unless you are running it, forget working within the system as life passes you by. The system does what it was designed to do, that is, enslave us. Nor should you expect any help from the middle class unless it is to run a soup kitchen so that their high-school children can list it on their resume to score admissions points for Harvard, Princeton, Yale—all while your poor high-school kids work at McExploitation to help the family. You want change? It does not come with a vote; that's simply naïve. For true liberty we need direct action even at the cost of our blood.

Revolt! synthesizes sociology, history, economics, and political science to demystify the workings of the system and openly call for militant direct action, as prescribed by none other than Thomas Jefferson, to end working-class misery. It champions radical ideology, societal education, independent media, and direct action to obtain direct political and economic democracy. Historically, working-class gains have been obtained through militant, often revolutionary, direct action. This was possible due to a core of radical leaders within the labor and civil rights movements. These leaders implemented a strategy of developing a radical counter ideology that challenged dominant capitalist ideology; promoted class consciousness and solidarity through grassroots societal education using their own media; and engaged in civil disobedience and self-defense against capitalist and state violence, including full-scale rebellion. It is through conflict that working-class gains are achieved rather than by appeals to the moral conscience of the powerful. It is a tribute to the effectiveness of direct action that the capitalist state has outlawed many of its forms, e.g., with no-strike contract clauses and right-to-work legislation such as New York State's Taylor Law which makes it illegal for public employees to strike, imposing hefty fines and prison terms if they do.

Who is the working class? Endless debates have sprouted regarding what exactly constitutes the working-class. Countless academics have sliced and diced, defined and redefined, this and related terms, to the point of meaninglessness. For this book we go back to basics by defining the working class as those who do not own sufficient productive property to be able to live an average lifestyle without being compelled to work.

While some workers are better compensated than others or given greater autonomy, the definition of a worker is clear: whether you are a doctor or a janitor, you are a worker if you must work to survive.

The book also uses interchangeably the terms "militant", "radical", and "revolutionary". There may be a wide spectrum of tactics and strategies that could be labeled as either militant or revolutionary. A militant may also advocate or not violent self-defense or violent direct action. A radical may advocate plant occupations or destruction of corporate property. A revolutionary may be such due to her ideology rather than actions. At the end, dissecting these terms into non-meaning, as many academics tend to do, is left up to them. My intention is to get things done and this will not happen by fancy academese but rather practical, reasoned thinking put into action. Radical is militant and revolution is radical.

Corporations, the rich, and government form a "circulation of elites" that manifests itself as monolithic power, therefore, these terms are used interchangeably. They are an extremely small percentage of the population ranging from 1% to 5% and all odds are this does not include YOU or me.

What about the shrinking middle class? They too are part of the working class; they just don't know it due to their extreme false class consciousness. These remnants of empowered bureaucratic workers known as the middle class and referred to as the "coordinator class" in anarchist economics are co-opted and brainwashed beyond salvation. Worse, they are fierce defendants of their upper-class masters who offer them crumbs of privilege and therefore might as well be forsaken as the lost petite bourgeois. They will never align themselves with the black mother from Paterson, New Jersey. Historically they have always betrayed the working class in one bourgeois revolution after another. They will only "assist" the poor to get credit for public service to either help them get into a Harvard, Princeton, or Yale, or to pad a resume for political office. Forget them—they will eventually join us when they are foreclosed, outsourced, and become uninsured.

Chapter one of this book explains why we need to force structural socioeconomic change rather than reregulation of capitalism for sustained prosperity and social justice. Specifically, an international capitalist regime has formed based on global segmentation of labor, financialization and neoliberal trade. Unlike its Fordist era counterpart, this one lacks a corresponding regime for consumption because it has outsourced production to low-wage authoritarian regions. This is resulting in inadequate purchasing power within developed nations, for whom global production is intended, creating the structural foundations of the global crisis. The economic collapse of 2008 occurred when the US consumer debt bubble that fueled consumption finally burst. The existing system is intensifying class contradictions embedded in productive private property relations and will lead to intensified downturns. Therefore, the only structural solution is not reform but fundamental reorganization of socioeconomic relations. However, this requires a new transnational labor-activist movement willing to fight capitalism's hegemony.

Chapter two establishes that to obtain egalitarianism, the legitimacy of capitalism must be challenged with a radical counter ideology disseminated among the working class. This radical counter ideology can only be spread through societal education (based on Paulo Freire's critical pedagogy) and mass media owned by the workers as in the past, demonstrated by the historical analysis of chapter three. Critical education is needed to cultivate class consciousness leading to solidarity and the understanding that direct action is the only meaningful weapon for change as in the past. Such action need not seek an immediate end or overthrow of government but strategic changes in the relations of production that would set in motion radical evolutionary change toward a society based on egalitarian principles. One such idea that I propose is the use of direct action to demand that all corporate boards of directors be comprised exclusively by worker and community representatives. This would lead to an intermediary period characterized by communal control of productive private property. It would also provide a real-life model and experience with new forms of societal organization, leading to stable evolutionary, epochal change. Other immediate demands through direct action would include universal, single-payer free health care, nationalization of all educational institutions and free education at all levels (and fundamental transformation of current curricula based on principles of critical pedagogy), universal free housing, and guaranteed food, utilities/services, and overall minimum living standards.

Based on historical analysis, chapter three demonstrates that the working class can obtain meaningful gains only through militant direct action modeled on the labor movement of the past. The history of the eight-hour workday is reviewed as a case study showing that it was won because of radical leaders who challenged existing legal institutional frameworks through societal education, radical ideology, direct action and violent resistance against state attacks. Positive changes did not occur politically, peacefully or voluntarily. Instead, oftentimes the threat of or use of violent resistance and even rebellion had preceded major concessions for the working class.

Chapter three also shows that the civil rights movement succeeded because of, rather than in spite of, radical leaders such as Malcom X, Stokely Carmichael, and Rob Williams, who advocated violent resistance and rebellion that forced the US government to move on civil rights. Had it not been for the real threat of revolution, nonviolent civil disobedience leaders may not have been taken seriously by the US government, which was forced to decide whether to deal with them voluntarily or risk continued open revolution. Let us not forget it was the Republicans and Dixie Democrats, including the Kennedy brothers, who stonewalled blacks on the passage of political reforms. Even after these reforms had been passed it was through on-the-ground direct action that the system finally began to enforce civil rights laws.

Having demonstrated what, why, and how can be accomplished with direct action and radical counter ideology, chapter four informs who the real looters of society are leading to the collapse of 2008. *Revolt!* shows through facts and figures, e.g., welfare versus "wealthfare" and government expenditures (including the mega bailouts for the hyper rich), how the current capitalist system legalizes looting by the hyper rich while jailing the poor whenever they shoplift a shirt to wear. In addition to exposing the hypocrisy of the legal system, the chapter also calls openly for organized resistance in a manner that would get the attention of the elite: organized mass lootings of major anti-working-class employers when they refuse to provide minimum standards such as health insurance and family wages. This brings the argument full circle and connects it to the same actions undertaken during the radical labor movement and the civil rights rebellion. Finally, the chapter aims at demonstrating to working-class people that laws are not made by the poor but by the rich to benefit themselves and, as such, we have a right to resist regardless of what the overlords label us. Second, there is no hope in appeals to government or to the middle class as these are equally deaf to the needs of the working class. Therefore, workers of the world can only depend on themselves and their strength as a global class to take what is rightfully theirs.

The conclusion provides a synopsis of the main arguments, and ends with a call to engage in individual involvement with grassroots organizations, becoming self-informed through alternative media outlets, and sharing this information with others so as to build a true movement from below for social justice. *Revolt!* also provides the reader with an opportunity to engage in action through the organization which inspired the author to take action: the Transformative Studies Institute, a scholar-activist graduate school in the making as a base of social movement

Introduction

building. Readers are directed to the website of this institution for more information at www.transformativestudies.org.

In global solidarity,
Dr. John Asimakopoulos

Notes

1. McLaren, Peter, Best, Steven, and Nocella II, Anthony J. (eds.). 2009. *Academic Repression: Reflections from the Academic Industrial Complex*. Oakland, CA: AK Press.
2. Ibid.

1

Kleptocracy Capitalism: Why Humpty Dumpty Must Always Fall

"The cheap prices of its commodities are the heavy artillery with which it batters down all Chinese walls."

Karl Marx

In 2007 the housing bubble burst, exposing pyramid schemes known as "securitized mortgage assets" which were financed by easy monetary policy[1] and neoliberal deregulation championed by Alan Greenspan. Consumer spending evaporated, the dollar fell, national debt skyrocketed, the unemployment rate jumped to over 10%—the highest in decades, the world's advanced economies slowed, and developing nations were devastated.

On September 8, 2008 the US government renationalized Fannie Mae and Freddie Mac, subjecting tax payers to $5.4 trillion in mortgage securities debt with a $200 billion capital injection upon the nationalization. The reason was to prevent a total meltdown of the housing market and of consumption in general. In earlier months the Federal Reserve had purchased $30 billion of securitized mortgage assets to make the acquisition of Bear Stearns by J.P. Morgan Chase possible and prevent a global collapse of financial markets. Many reports routinely announced statistics with the comment *"worse than the Great Depression."* The International Monetary Fund (IMF) lost credibility and is in its worst financial health in years. This, together with a global credit crunch and energy geopolitics, is redefining global relationships, one of which is the slow abandonment of the World Trade Organization (WTO) after the collapse of negotiations in 2008. According to the Congressional Budget Office, as of summer 2009 the US approved $787 billion in stimulus spending, with trillions in additional commitments and calls for a second package to save capitalism which will be paid for by neo-serf taxpayers.

As expected, the government reacted by saving the very corporations responsible for triggering the collapse. However, these financial corporations were not the cause of the crisis. Rather, they expedited the normal workings of the capitalist system after a thirty-year period of stagnant and even declining real income for the bottom 80% of the population. Many people today do not realize that the Great Depression of the 1930s was not the first nor will it be the last. Throughout capitalism's history there have been numerous depressions and panics lasting years, with equally disastrous outcomes as during the 1930s. For example, the Panic of 1819 lasted five years; the Panic and Depression of 1837 lasted six years; and the Panic of 1873 and the ensuing Long Depression lasted from 1873–96 and was known as the Great Depression until the 1930s. As Marxist and even capitalist economists have shown, downturns and depressions are a structural reality of capitalism. Consequently, the working class is brainwashed to accept and even defend a system that enslaves them while crashing repeatedly.

As many have argued, these business cycles and crises are a normal consequence of capitalism's contradictions, namely overproduction and underconsumption. This refers to wages being inadequate to support a sufficient level of aggregate demand, leading to a self-reinforcing downward cycle of businesses slashing production, with a consequent loss of employment and income with which to purchase output leading to new rounds of cutbacks. Here is where the brilliance of the economist John Maynard Keynes and Keynesian economics[2] came in proposing government stimulus to jump-start the economy—until the next crisis.

Depressions consequently are nothing new. What is new is capitalism's most recent great transformation into a truly global system of integrated finance, production, and consumption. As a result, the normal contradictions found at the national level have been globalized further and deeper than ever before. This has the effect of intensifying capitalism's normal contradictions with the potential of increasingly deeper and protracted downturns. So what is new with capitalism and how exactly does it (not) work?

The emerging production model known as globalization is reexamined using the institutional framework of Social Structures of Accumulation (SSA). According to SSA theory, multiple social and historical factors, rather than mechanistic economics, determine economic growth. Specifically, capitalists invest on expectations of return. These expectations are shaped by external economic, as well as political and ideological conditions. This external environment is referred to as the SSA, which not only determines economic expansion, but also the class distribution of economic gains. Important features of the institutional environment are the system of money and credit, the pattern of state involvement in the economy, and the structure of class conflict.[3]

The structure of class conflict is of particular importance because it determines the shape of institutional arrangements and whether they will be conducive to investment. SSA also holds that expansionary periods eventually end due to institutional relations becoming ossified, relative to the demands of new economic realities.[4] This is the Marxist argument of the relations of production[5] (institutional relations) becoming fetters to the forces of production[6] (industrial capacity).[7] Lastly, this approach views the development of each SSA "as historically contingent, its internal unity as historically contingent, and its disintegration as historically contingent."[8]

Furthermore, historically contingent class conflicts and inter-capitalist rivalries result in an uneven process of growth and accumulation. In addition, there is unevenness built into the system exemplified by the business cycle and Kondratieff long waves.[9] In turn, with each business cycle there results a greater concentration of capital and a reduction in the size of the capitalist class. Now a global SSA has formed based on financialization, neoliberal trade, and a new global segmentation of labor resulting from, and intensifying, the defeat of working classes in developed nations. But as the historical process of capital concentration is intensifying, occurring at the international versus national level, the fundamental mechanics of capitalism remain unchanged. However, this presents a *qualitative* break from the past in that corporations have severed the flow of a national business cycle by outsourcing *production* to nations with preindustrial labor and civil rights conditions for cheap disciplined workers while depending on market-based *consumption* in advanced nations. This leads to reductions in purchasing power without a mechanism to restore income flows back to the worker-consumers of developed nations. Consequently, the class contradictions of the new system will result in continued global economic stagnation, if not collapse, without real new growth accumulation. The reason is that the new regime of global production lacks a corresponding regime for consumption. Inevitably this will cause stagnation due to the classic contradiction of overproduction and underconsumption emanating from capitalist private property relations. Therefore, a structural solution is not reform but altering private productive property relations[10] toward libertarian socialist forms of societal organization, allowing for the uninterrupted flow of production and consumption (market clearing).

For the purposes of this book, the working class includes any person or household that does not own adequate means of production[11] to be able to live at an average lifestyle without being compelled to work. "Outsourcing" refers to the transfer of production from developed to developing regions and the strategic decision to make new investments in the latter. It is also assumed that corporations reflect the interests of the upper class which owns them, thus the two terms will be used interchangeably.[12] The upper class controls the state which protects and promotes its interests. Market clearing occurs when purchasing power allows aggregate demand to equal output (there are no market shortages or surpluses). "Neoliberalism" and "globalization" refer to free trade and capital flows, outsourcing, anti-labor policies, privatization and deregulation, upper-class tax cuts, and cuts in social spending. As known, the principle of "self-organization" refers to a form of direct democracy (people representing themselves), while "self-direction" refers to worker-owned and-operated collective production. Last, libertarian socialism, which includes self-organization and self-direction, is a social system which believes in freedom of action and thought and free will, in which the producers possess both political power and the means of production and distribution.

COMPONENTS OF THE NEW GLOBAL SSA

Given the declining rate of profit since the 1970s within developed nations, capitalism has pursued surplus value[13] through globalization.[14] But is this the beginning of a new mode of production?[15] The answer is no because these changes are more accurately described as evolutions of a fundamentally capitalist mode of production.[16] Rather, we are witnessing the solidification of a new US-led global SSA, or "hegemonic regime" in the language of political scientists, based on three emerging regimes. The first is the financial regime based on the World Bank and International Monetary Fund (IMF) functioning as (de)regulatory institutions for the global economy.[17] The second is a neoliberal trade regime expressed by the WTO and Free Trade Agreements (FTAs).[18] The third involves globally segmented labor markets[19] made possible by, and intensifying, the defeat of national working classes. The origins of these regimes can be traced back to developed nations, in particular the hegemonic United States and to a lesser degree, the European Union. In fact, we now have the emergence of *global managers* consisting of transnational corporations and banks, the WTO, the World Bank and IMF, and the G-7.[20]

The Financial Regime

The formation of the new financial regime centered on the IMF, World Bank, and transnational banks can be traced to the 1980s. Its creation came out of the collapse of Bretton Woods[21] in the 1970s. At that time, transnational banks were forming, providing offshore tax havens without controls on capital flows for transnational corporations. The banks accumulated massive reserves from corporate accounts which were then lent to developing nations, laying the foundation for the 1980s debt crises. These developments and corporate behavior were also a major cause for the demise of the Bretton Woods regime (which had institutionalized the old colonial relations) and financial deregulation, e.g., of capital flows and currency exchange rates, causing the Mexican currency crisis in 1994 and Asia in 1997. In the wake of the 1980s debt crises, the role of the World Bank and IMF changed *qualitatively* by adopting neoliberal principles leading to the formation of new financial and trade regimes. The adoption of neoliberal ideology by these institutions was assured given that the United States has 16.79% of the vote at the IMF[22] and 16.38% at the World Bank[23]—shares multiple times more than that of any other single nation. Combined, the United States and European Union have 48.88% of the vote at the IMF[24] and 44.94% at the World Bank;[25] and traditionally the World Bank is headed by an American and the IMF by a European.

Some scholars have argued that the financial regime is not new.[26] Rather, it is a continuation of forces dating to the formation of Bretton Woods when the financial sector was requesting policies that are associated today with neoliberalism, such as free capital flows. It is no surprise that financial or any other capital was opposed to regulation that it did not control. What is important is that Bretton Woods did not include these demands. Therefore the liberalization of capital flows is more properly dated to the 1980s although it has its origins in the prior system. Interestingly, Panitch and Gindin seem to acknowledge this qualitative shift: "The impact on American financial institutions of inflation, low real interest rates and stagnant profits in the 1970s accelerated the *qualitative transformations* [italics added] of these years, which increasingly ran up against the old New Deal banking regulations. ... This was what prompted the global 'financial services revolution.'"[27]

Specifically, the first major shift occurred when in its *World Development Report 1980*, the World Bank changed the definition of development from "nationally managed economic growth" to "participation in the world market."[28] This was a move away from what in essence were protectionist policies (nationally managed economic growth) utilized by developing nations toward neoliberal global trade (meaning capital mobility) controlled by and privileging transnational corporations. Second, the World Bank and IMF went from providing development assistance in the form of project loans to reorganizing the economies of poor nations in crisis through policy or structural adjustment loans. For example, when poor nations are forced to seek loans from the IMF (as a lender of last resort) they must agree to neoliberal reorganization of their economy—especially privatization—before obtaining assistance from the World Bank and transnational banks.[29] In addition to privatization of state resources, these measures which reflect the 1980s Thatcherite Reaganite ideology include severe reductions in public spending, currency devaluation, and wage reductions to attract "foreign investment" as a result of decreased export prices.[30]

Therefore, the emerging financial regime is designed to facilitate global capital mobility in search of profits via cheap labor. The importance of capital mobility and privatization is that it makes possible the financing of production and ownership of national resources in developing regions. This is demonstrated by the record level of net Foreign Direct Investment (FDI) inflows to China which have intensified upon its WTO entry in 2001.[31] In fact, the implementation of such policies has been followed by intensification in FDI flows to extremely poor nations given no restrictions on profit repatriation. Prior to such liberalization, nations imposed restrictions on the levels of FDI flows and foreign ownership of domestic industries to maintain control over their economies. However, this made it difficult for transnational corporations to engage in their investment strategies. More important than rock-bottom prices for national resources, the regime secures the repatriation of profits from production in developing nations. The threat of capital mobility also makes it possible for corporations to continuously extract concessions from developing host nations and to discipline uncooperative governments.[32] Finally, corporations reap tax benefits with international shell accounting and offshore banking which the financial regime make possible.[33]

Is this a stable regime and what about inter-state rivalries? In terms of interstate rivalries, the financial regime is the most stable out of the three which constitute the emerging SSA. This is true despite the collapse of 2008 because it institutionalizes US global financial interests tying the economies of other nations to it. The globalization of finance has included the *Americanization* of finance, and the deepening and extension of financial markets has become more than ever fundamental to the reproduction and universalization of American power.[34] However, this is not sufficient to stabilize the global system of which financialization is but only a component. More specifically, as argued by Frank:

> financial instruments have been ever further compounding already compounded interest on the real properties in which their stake and debts are based, which has contributed to the spectacular growth of this financial world. Nonetheless, the financial pyramid that we see in all its splendour and brilliance, especially in its centre at Uncle Sam's home, still sits on top of a real world producer-merchant-consumer base, even if the financial one also provides credit for these real world transactions. ... As world consumer of last resort ... Uncle Sam performs this important function in the present-day global political-economic division of labour. Everybody else produces and needs to export while Uncle Sam consumes and needs to import. ... [a significant reduction in US consumption] may involve a wholesale reorganisation of the world political economy presently run by Uncle Sam.[35]

Therefore, the Achilles heel of the system remains consumption. This is true even if nations such as China and Japan have no choice but to participate in the financial regime through purchases of T-bills to prop up the value of the dollar and thus US consumption and imports. In other words, even a global financial regime is dependent on a balance between production and consumption, leading us back to purchasing power and aggregate demand as will be addressed.

The Neoliberal Trade Regime

Corporations, however, needed another element present in order to take full advantage of globalized production. While the financial regime secures capital mobility, the global trade regime centered on the WTO and other FTAs is needed to secure mobility of production. The blueprint was the 1994 North American Free Trade Agreement (NAFTA). NAFTA allowed the free flow of goods and investment *but not of people* between an industrialized high-wage region and a developing one with extremely low wages. According to Scott et al.:

> NAFTA ... provided investors with a unique set of guarantees designed to stimulate foreign direct investment and the movement of factories within the hemisphere, especially from the United States to Canada and Mexico. Furthermore, no protections were contained in

the core of the agreement to maintain labor or environmental standards. As a result, NAFTA tilted the economic playing field in favor of investors, and against workers and the environment, resulting in a hemispheric "race to the bottom" in wages and environmental quality.[36]

It was predicted by proponents that NAFTA would lead to a US trade surplus with Mexico. Instead, from 1993 to 2004, it rapidly led to a $107.3 billion trade deficit and a loss of 1,015,291 US jobs.[37]

The establishment of the WTO in 1995 extended these dynamics to a global scale. For example, the US trade deficit with pre-WTO China averaged $9 billion per year from 1997 to 2001.[38] When China entered the WTO in 2001, the deficit began to average $38 billion per year from 2001 to 2006.[39] As a result of these investment flows:

> The rise in the U.S. trade deficit with China between 1997 and 2006 has displaced production that could have supported 2,166,000 U.S. jobs. Most of these jobs (1.8 million) have been lost since China entered the WTO in 2001. Between 1997 and 2001, growing trade deficits displaced an average of 101,000 jobs per year … Since China entered the WTO in 2001, job losses increased to an average of 441,000 per year.[40]

Furthermore, between 1948 and 1970 there were only six FTAs, thirty-four from 1971 to 1991, but after the establishment of the WTO in 1995 the number of FTAs reached 181 by 2002 spreading neoliberal trade far and wide (Table 1). The WTO itself is the successor to the 1948 General Agreement on Tariffs and Trade (GATT) which the United States created as an alternative to the International Trade Organization because it included the UN's Declaration of Human Rights such as full employment, social security, etc. Consequently, the WTO reflects the interests of its creator and dominant state(s). As with all past global systems of accumulation, the WTO is technically an independent institution (to give it the semblance of legitimacy) which in practice is controlled by the hegemonic United States and to a lesser degree the elites of other developed nations.

This neoliberal trade regime allows corporations to safely move production around the globe in search of low labor costs and financial incentives without fear of tariffs or barriers in order to boost historically declining profits. For example, the Organisation for Economic Co-operation and Development (OECD) estimates that 20% of US outward direct investment is protected by FTAs, 43% for Canada, and over 60% for the UK.[41] Even Japan, which has only recently accelerated its FTA memberships, has 12% of its outward FDI protected.[42] In addition to lowering transaction costs for globalized production, FTAs also guarantee that once the goods are produced in low-wage regions they can be exported unhindered into developed nations like the United States for market-based consumption. Barriers to trade would have made this unprofitable, thus limiting the extent of globalization.

Table 1. Total Number of Regional Trade Agreements 1948–2002

YEAR OF ENTRY INTO FORCE	NUMBER OF REGIONAL TRADE AGREEMENTS	YEAR OF ENTRY INTO FORCE	NUMBER OF REGIONAL TRADE AGREEMENTS	YEAR OF ENTRY INTO FORCE	NUMBER OF REGIONAL TRADE AGREEMENTS
1948	0	1968	5	1988	29
1949	0	1969	5	1989	31
1950	0	1970	6	1990	31
1951	0	1971	8	1991	34
1952	0	1972	8	1992	43
1953	0	1973	15	1993	56
1954	0	1974	15	1994	65
1955	0	1975	15	1995	80
1956	0	1976	17	1996	91
1957	0	1977	21	1997	110
1958	2	1978	21	1998	129
1959	2	1979	21	1999	141
1960	3	1980	21	2000	156
1961	4	1981	24	2001	167
1962	4	1982	24	2002	181
1963	4	1983	25		
1964	4	1984	26		
1965	4	1985	27		
1966	4	1986	28		
1967	4	1987	28		

Source: Global Policy Forum, http://www.globalpolicy.org

Moreover, FTA rules are typically designed in secret by corporations and their governments, often with little or no participation of any citizen, environmental, or labor groups, as with the WTO proceedings.[43] Not surprisingly, the trading rules disproportionately privilege capitalist interests, which pit high-income workers of developed regions against those of underdeveloped regions through outsourcing and Export Processing Zones (EPZs).[44] For example, Mexican real wages have remained flat despite NAFTA's promises, as employment increased together with declines in US jobs and real wages:

> Mexican employment did increase, but much of it in low-wage "maquiladora" [EPZ] industries, which the promoters of NAFTA promised would disappear. ... the share of jobs with no security, no benefits, and no future expanded. The continued willingness every year of hundreds of thousands of Mexican citizens to risk their lives crossing the border to the United States because they cannot make a living at home is in itself testimony to the failure of NAFTA to deliver on the promises of its promoters.[45]

Globally Segmented Labor Markets

These policies shift national labor market segmentation[46] to a new artificially created *global segmentation of labor* without corresponding limitations on capital flows. The origins of the new labor regime can be traced back to the 1980s when the United States had to contain inflation to stem capital outflows and balance the international financial system. At the time, taming inflation meant increasing interest rates through the Volcker shock (by reducing the money supply and later increasing Federal rates) and containing wage-led inflation from a moribund US labor and civil rights movement. The latter was achieved by crushing the remnants of the labor movement as when Reagan fired the air traffic controllers. This cleared the way for financial capital to expand its global outreach (by securing international confidence in the value of the dollar) and its merging with production capital. According to Panitch and Gindin:

> the Volcker shock's contribution to the new priority of "breaking inflationary expectations" in the early '80s depended on something more fundamental still. ... the real issue was not so much finding the right monetary policy, as restructuring class relations. Breaking inflationary expectations could not be achieved without defeating the working class's aspirations and its collective capacity to act ...

Volcker would later say that "the most important single action of the administration in helping the anti-inflation fight was defeating the air traffic controllers strike." It was on this basis that the American state regained the confidence of Wall Street and financial markets more generally. This proved pivotal to the reconstitution of the American empire by unleashing the new form of social rule subsequently labeled "neoliberalism" – promoting the expansion of markets and using their discipline to remove the barriers to accumulation that earlier democratic gains had achieved.[47]

Although the new labor accord had been initiated by Reagan repressing US workers in the 1980s, it could not be fully developed into globally segmented labor markets without first the financial regime to secure capital mobility (1980s) and second the neoliberal free trade regime (1995) to secure mobility of production but not of people. For this reason the emergence of globally segmented labor markets can be dated to 1994–95 with the establishment of NAFTA and the WTO, the final element in the equation. In essence, neoliberal globalization and the emergence of globally segmented labor markets, reinstitutionalize the old Bretton Woods core–periphery relations which it had institutionalized in turn from the pre–World War I colonial system. Effectively, the world's poor are trapped in regions of absolute-poverty-wages, creating a modern serfdom. According to Satterfield:

> The internal 'logic' of the new SSA is that of a *core-periphery* model of accumulation. It can be successfully adopted by a subset of national economies (the core) [i.e. US, EU, and Japan], but these, in turn, require the existence of a periphery of non-participating economies from which they are able to import unemployment as a worker discipline device [which means that] a *credible* threat to relocate production is necessary.[48]

It follows that corporations also use the threat of outsourcing to discipline developed-region workers by arguing that their wages and benefits are too high and thus not globally competitive. This in turn accelerates the downward spiral in labor standards. However, one could argue that the problem is low wages in poor regions that need to be raised. This is why many scholars and activists have argued in favor of *fair trade*[49] rather than free trade.[50]

More importantly, global segmentation of labor markets presents a *qualitative* change in that it institutionalizes and intensifies a 1970s labor accord based on defeated national working classes by updating the traditional core-periphery divide of colonialism and neo-colonialism. This creates high-income regions (Figure 1) of *democratic market-based consumption*, where consumers are given greater sovereignty and consumption opportunities. However, as workers, they experience flat real wages, increasing inequality, and the erosion of social safety nets such as pensions, health-care benefits, and job security.[51] Low-income regions of *authoritarian production* such as China are also created, where the great majority of people remain subsistence-wage consumers. For example, "it has been estimated that wages in China would be 47 to 85 percent higher in the absence of labor repression."[52] All too often these workers experience flat and extremely low incomes, violations of basic human and labor rights, and sweatshop conditions, while independent monitors and the media are prohibited in such factories and EPZs.[53] The National Labor Committee (NLC) made note of the following:

> The lack of worker rights, especially the core internationally recognized labor rights to freedom of association, to organize independent unions and to bargain collectively, is the single greatest reason that China's factory workers are being left behind. The tens of millions of rural migrants working in China's export factories are certainly one of the pillars – if not the most significant one – supporting China's surging economy, the fastest growing in modern history. Yet the workers' wages have remained largely stagnant over the last decade.[54]

Furthermore, although the Bureau of Labor Statistics does not track Chinese wages, it estimated the hourly factory compensation in China to be sixty-four cents, including wages, benefits, and social insurance.[55] By contrast, in 2004 the hourly factory compensation in Mexico and Brazil was $2.50 and $3.03 respectively, compared to $21.90 in Japan, $23.17 in the United States, $23.89 in France, $24.71 in the United Kingdom, and $32.53 in Germany.[56] In addition, wages for China, Mexico, and Brazil have remained relatively flat since the 1990s as other parts of the world have been able to offer even cheaper labor. For example, the average hourly wage for apparel workers in Guatemala is thirty-seven to fifty cents, twenty to thirty cents in India, and ten cents in Indonesia, with Bangladesh coming in at a mere one cent.[57] Consequently the promises of NAFTA and other FTA promoters that these agreements would increase real earnings in developing member nations have been shown to be false.

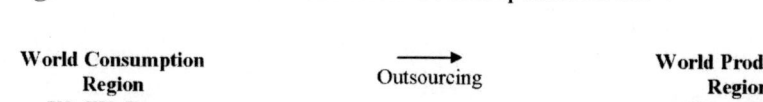

Figure 1. The Global Production-Consumption Model

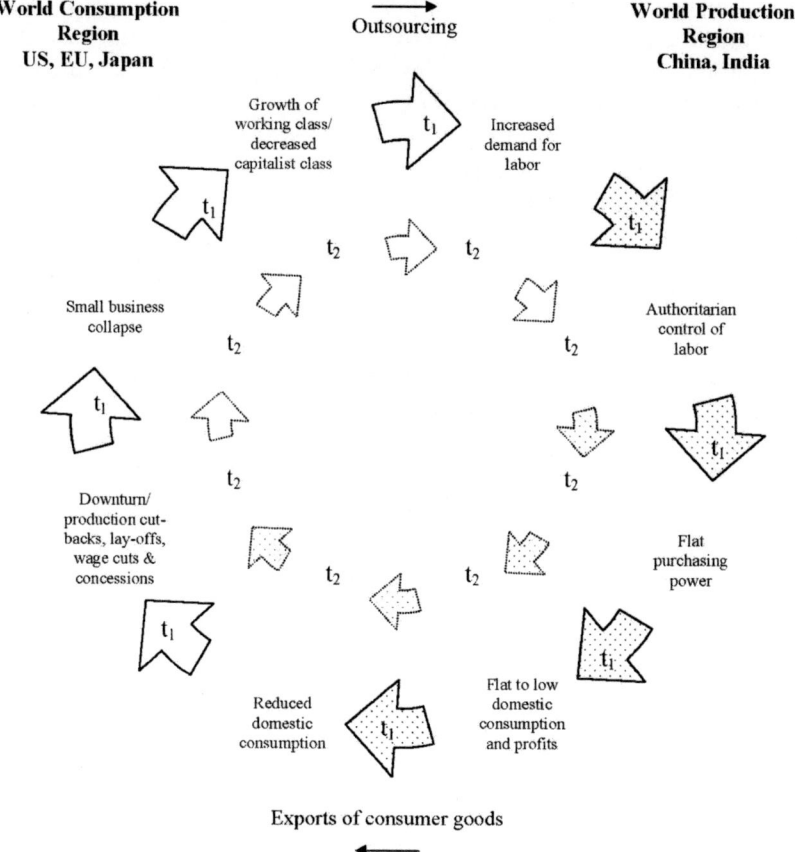

On the consumption side, the average pair of Puma sneakers retails for $70 in the United States, giving Puma a gross profit of $34.09.[58] However, these shoes are produced in Pou Yuen, China for a total labor cost of $1.16, with the worker getting an average take-home pay of thirty-five cents per hour.[59] Clearly, the cost savings are kept almost entirely by the corporation, rather than being passed on to the US consumer. Moreover, regardless of the purchasing power parities, Chinese and developing-world workers cannot afford these consumer goods. The worker mentioned above would have to work 200 hours, or five forty-hour weeks, for one pair of shoes that she produced with about three hours of labor!

In other words, low-wage regions are simply segregated labor markets for production that is intended for the developed regions as indicated by US-China trade flows.

In general, the macroeconomic picture that the three regimes are painting is very clear. The role of the IMF and World Bank changed to that of facilitators of capital mobility by the 1980s with the collapse of the Bretton Woods accord. In the 1990s, the neoliberal trade regime began to solidify with the transformation of GATT into the WTO (1995) and the formation of NAFTA (1994) a year earlier. Once the basic neoliberal trade structure was established it set the stage for the formation of additional FTAs.

Having secured the mobility of capital and goods through the trade and financial regimes, corporations then began to outsource investment into developing nations for extremely low labor costs while suppressing workers at home. This explains why from 1993 to 1998 the top three recipients of FDI among developing nations were China (25.7%), Brazil (7.6%), and Mexico (6.5%), with India also gaining in recent years.[60] The preceding nations all have very large labor pools in absolute poverty combined with relatively stable political structures. As a result, 2004 net FDI inflows to China reached record levels at $53 billion, while net FDI outflows from the United States exceeded $145 billion compared to previous net FDI inflows of $11.3 billion in 1990.[61]

As FDI inflows to low-wage regions reached record levels, so did America's trade deficit, as corporations shipped back the output of outsourced production to developed regions for consumption. For example, the US trade deficit with China reached $201 billion in 2005, compared to the pre-WTO levels of $10.4 billion in 1990 and $6 billion in 1985.[62] The declining growth rates of real Gross Domestic Product (GDP) per capita in developed nations is the mirror image of these trade deficits as corporations relocate production (and now services) to developing ones, with the most significant drop after the 1990s when the emerging regimes began to solidify (Table 2). Theoretically the privileged position of the United States in the global system could allow it to experience perpetual trade deficits that nations like China have no choice but to accept.[63] This is possible given that the international reserve and trade currency is the US dollar. Thus, the United States can purchase global goods denominated in its own currency by printing money at a cost of a few cents for paper and ink.[64] However, these deficits have real consequence for US workers:

> Growth in trade deficits with China has reduced demand for goods produced in every region of the United States ... Workers displaced by trade from the manufacturing sector have been shown to have particular difficulty in securing comparable employment elsewhere in the economy. More than one-third of workers displaced from manufacturing drop out of the labor force ... Average wages of those who secured re-employment fell 11% to 13%. Trade-related job displacement pushes many workers out of good jobs in manufacturing and other trade-related industries, often into lower-paying industries and frequently out of the labor market.[65]

Such outsourcing has contributed to flat and even reduced real wages for the US working-class as incomes of the upper class rise, leading to growing inequality. For example, the Gini ratios[66] for households in America were 0.397 in 1967, 0.419 in 1985, 0.450 in 1995, and 0.466 in 2004.[67] Furthermore, these shifts lead to reduced purchasing power and hence, aggregate demand. Consequently, corporate profits have also been declining. The profit rate for the 500 largest US transnational corporations was 7.71 and 7.15 percent in the 1950s and 1960s respectively when the Fordist[68] model was operative.[69] Profit rates dropped to 5.3 and 2.29% in the 1980s and 1990s, while they were only at 1.32% from 2000–2002.[70] This trend was found to be identical in fact for the largest transnational corporations, regardless of their national origin. From 2001 to 2005 profit rates began to rise reaching 4.6% in the non-financial sector.[71] This was attributed to corporations keeping productivity growth of 3.1% per year, resulting in flat real wages for workers that saw compensation rise only 0.6% per year.[72] Corporations were able to keep wages flat despite productivity growth due to the workings of the emerging neoliberal model.[73] More so, corporations are extracting ever greater surplus value from workers in low-wage regions. This is fundamentally what underscores increases in corporate profits since 2001 when globalization was solidifying instead of innovations and productive investments.

In other words, globalization has constructed a finely tuned system that focuses on the efficiency of SSAs related to production. But economic activity is based on a production-consumption model and it is consumption that globalization is undermining. In the typical workings of a national business cycle, capitalist accumulation is equivalent to a siphoning-off of surplus value and thus purchasing power away from the working class into the pockets of the capitalists. But unless the capitalists invest that wealth in activities that generate jobs and adequate income, the economy will stagnate due to overproduction and underconsumption.

Here Keynesianism's importance becomes clear in that to end a downturn, government spending is needed to spark consumption and thus market clearing. This is largely why supply-side or trickle-down economics has been proven ineffective as demonstrated by the Reagan and Bush administrations, echoing Marx's critique of Say's Law.[74] Namely, giving the capitalist class tax breaks, dismantling social safety nets, and creating low-paid flexible workforces add up to capitalist windfalls without guarantees that these savings will be invested in high-income, job-generating businesses.[75]

Table 2. Average Yearly Percent Growth of Real GDP per Capita (using PPP in 2005 dollars)

	1960–69	1970–79	1980–89	1990–99	2000–08
US	3.33	2.53	2.49	1.99	1.21
UK	2.25	2.31	2.8	2.11	1.86
France	4.56	3.3	1.83	1.36	0.97
Germany*	3.46	2.8	1.79	1.54	1.22
Japan	9.13	3.44	3.23	0.81	1.2

Author's calculations based on data from the US Department of Labor, 2009
(*Data for Germany for years before 1991 pertain to the former West Germany)

As Figure 1 demonstrates, globalization is short-circuiting the income flow in the developed regions between production and consumption more so than nationally based business cycles. Thus, globalization with its combination of an SSA for democratic market-based mass consumption (upon which it depends) and the SSA of authoritarian organization of production is siphoning off purchasing power from producers and consumers in the developed regions at a greater rate. "The result tends to be a high profit/stagnant wage expansion [for developed nations] that faces a contradiction between the conditions for creation of surplus value and those necessary for its realization."[76]

TOWARD COLLAPSE: A GLOBAL SSA WITHOUT INCOME?

The question for scholars today is whether globalization can increase productivity, which would raise wages, consumption, and the living standards of society as a whole (as has historically been the case under the Fordist model). However, this new global SSA is not capable of sustaining an expansionary period.[77] This is supported by the data on declining or flat GDP growth rates for the world's five largest economies (Table 2). Although the national working classes have been defeated since the 1970s, the capitalist global economy still has the normal contradictions found at the national level. Namely, regardless of the global financial and trading systems' stability and the increased rate of exploitation[78] through segmented international labor markets, a sale must be made before any profits are realized. If consumers' purchasing power is insufficient to clear markets, then stagnation is inevitable.

This is true because the mode of capitalist accumulation and thus economic growth depends on market-based consumption leading to Marxist critiques of overproduction and underconsumption.[79] Specifically, 86% of global goods and services are consumed by the wealthiest 20% of the world's population, generally in developed nations, especially the United States.[80] This implies that the production of the new global SSA depends on consumption primarily by the United States followed by the European Union and Japan.[81] Thus, although the financial system may be stable according to some, the overall global SSA, of which it is a component, is not given a severely defeated US working class.[82]

Could high US consumption needed by the global system be derived from shared productivity gains[83] between capital and labor? As noted, the answer is *no*; businesses have kept virtually all of the productivity gains.[84] What is even more troubling is that the gains themselves were derived not by technologically induced productivity growth, but by corporate savings, compliments of flat wages and a disciplined contingent labor force due to neoliberal restructuring of the economy.[85] Thus by definition it would be impossible to talk of shared productivity gains between labor and capital when they are derived at the expense of the former. Therefore, the historical trend of shared productivity gains that was expressed in the past Fordist expansionary SSA is no longer operative. Yet Americans continued to consume at high levels. "Here we arrive at the nub of the contradiction of accumulation in a neoliberal institutional structure. How can consumer spending continue to rise rapidly while real wages are repressed?"[86] For example, from 2000 to 2005 US consumption was increasing faster than growth in disposable personal income (Table 3).

The answer is debt. The growth of the 1980s and 1990s was fueled in large part by consumer credit/debt and government deficit spending.[87] The disappearing US middle class maintained its high consumption levels through debt.[88] As real wages started to stagnate from the 1970s, credit became easier to obtain. Growth in the mid-1990s was fueled partially by the wealth effect[89] of the stock market bubble, especially in technologies.[90] Most of the growth, though, was accounted for by consumer spending due to low interest rates making borrowing more affordable. For example, in 2003 the real average credit card debt per household reached $9,000, up from $4,000 in 1990.[91] Once consumers maxed out their credit cards at historic levels, new sources of debt continued to emerge, such as home equity loans that also reached historic levels.

Table 3. Growth Rates of Disposable Personal Income, Consumption, and Saving, 2000–2005

	2000	2001	2002	2003	2004	2005
Disposable personal income	4.8	1.9	3.1	2.4	3.4	1.4
Consumption	4.7	2.5	2.7	2.9	3.9	3.5
Gross Domestic Product	3.7	0.8	1.6	2.7	4.2	3.5
Personal saving as a percentage of disposable personal income	2.3	1.8	2.4	2.1	1.8	-0.4

Source: Kotz 2006: 26

In 2001 a severe recession was avoided thanks to continued strength in consumer spending. This was partially due to the temporary effect of the Bush tax cuts which benefited some middle-income but mostly upper-income households.[92] Most of the consumer spending, however, was accounted for by still-growing household debt. From 2003 to 2007, the US economy was driven by a continued rise in consumer spending despite flat incomes (Table 3). This spending had been financed by historically low interest rates given the glut of liquidity and credit by the Fed's easy monetary policy, contributing to the housing bubble. The illusion of wealth generated by the housing bubble, coupled with low interest rates and flat incomes, led to an explosion of home equity loans. For example, home equity loans in 1990 amounted to $150 billion versus over $300 billion in 1998 and $439 billion in 2006, while overall household debt (including credit cards and mortgages) as a percentage of after-tax income went from 30% in 1950 to over 90% in 2000 and 120% by 2005.[93] Thus, the middle class treated debt as income to sustain an unsustainable level of consumption while the working class depends on debt to get by, given stagnant and even declining real income. Therefore, the question remains how goods and services produced under globalization are going to be consumed as US consumer debt is maxed out, the equity bubble burst, and interest rates rise in the wake of the 2007 housing meltdown. Interestingly, this new domestic debt regime became possible thanks to the deregulation of the financial sector in the 1980s.

> The legislation facilitating competition in the financial services sector was also designed to expand consumer credit markets. The American working and middle classes maintained their standards of living by working longer hours and going into debt. They often re-mortgaged their homes to do so.[94]

This is also the basis of the argument that although some financial data may indicate a good national economy, they do so by excluding large swaths of the population. In other words, when it comes to distribution there are increasingly two separate worlds of haves and have-nots. "A mode of unequal growth [was established] in the mid-1980s, by which time it had become clear that income polarization and the associated phenomenon of the 'disappearing middle' of the employment distribution were structural rather than merely cyclical processes."[95] Ultimately, however, the global SSA cannot avoid the problem of inadequate demand since massive global production also requires massive market-based consumption. Consequently, globalization is the realization of the classic problem of overproduction and underconsumption.

REFORM VERSUS STRUCTURAL SOLUTIONS TO BOOM AND BUST

The problem is that globalization is developing the forces of production beyond the limits of the existing relations of production.[96] Therefore the current relations of production are becoming "fetters" to the full realization of the new productive forces. Stated differently, the emerging global SSA lacks the necessary mechanism for consumption which can result in severe economic downturns. One solution would be to apply Keynesian stimulus policies on a global scale. Ironically, this does not seem feasible because the neoliberal ideology behind globalization includes privatization, minimal government spending, and tax cuts. These policies result in undermining the fiscal ability of states to engage in large-scale Keynesian spending. In fact, during the aftermath of the 2008 financial collapse, many European governments, including Ireland, the United Kingdom, Greece, and Spain, slashed their budgets instead of increasing them to stimulate the economy. The justification was to trim deficits in the midst of the greatest depression since 1930. Unfortunately, even if governments increased spending, it would not resolve the class contradictions inherent in the capitalist mode of production as it relates to distribution and purchasing power.

Another alternative proposed by theorists is to promote re-regulation of national economies. For example, Harrison and Bluestone[97] argued that "red-hot" growth would be the best way to reduce inequality. They proposed a Main Street versus Wall Street model of Keynesian high-wage, pro-union, and anti-poverty programs to stimulate aggregate demand. They also advocated New Growth Theory, favoring supply-side growth through technological innovation to spur productivity growth. This, though, is not possible for the same reasons that prohibit a global Keynesian strategy. In addition, technologically driven productivity growth has not worked either.[98] As mentioned earlier, growth in the 1990s and early 2000 was driven by savings from a low-paid and disciplined contingency workforce made possible by outsourcing and anti-labor neoliberal policies. Furthermore, almost all productivity gains in the past years have been kept by businesses.

Others have proposed a re-regulation of the economy by government to balance the power between capitol and labor.[99] This suggestion was based on the observation that stagnation was caused when either capital or labor obtained an upper hand. In periods when capital had the advantage, it led to low wages and a flexible workforce, causing stagnation due to inadequate aggregate demand. In periods when labor had the advantage, it led to higher wages, lower profit margins, and stagnation due to a profit squeeze.[100] However, the capitalists' control of the state is part of the problem. In addition, it must be tacitly acknowledged that capital will always have a built-in advantage in that it owns the means of production. And although not overtly stated, it is implied that private productive property *is* the problem.

Another important fact is underscored by the argument of a profit squeeze.[101] Even if labor obtains an upper hand through revitalized movements and pro-labor government policies, it still would not provide a solution. Instead, this would lead to a temporary illusion of prosperity and ephemeral gains. This is because it would inevitably result in a profit squeeze, thus recession and a realignment of class power anew. Such a seesaw between inadequate aggregate demand and a profit squeeze will continue as long as class conflict takes place within a capitalist framework.

A third possible solution is that corporations voluntarily increase wages while cutting prices for goods and services. But this is another way of saying that the rate of exploitation be reduced, which hits the problem at its heart: namely, capitalist relations in production and consumption. This in fact would be the natural conclusion of all the policies discussed above. Thus, all of the suggestions by various theorists, let alone government policies, are ultimately unworkable in that they do not state what is clear: stagnation is caused structurally by private ownership of the means of production. Therefore, their policy suggestions are aimed at softening the natural outcomes of capitalism's class contradictions, while maintaining the capitalist mode of production. This point becomes more important if this new capitalism includes the normalization of ever-deeper crises and growing domestic and global inequalities which many argue should be accepted as here to stay.[102] Sadly, the historical record has proven that severe downturns are a normal structural element of capitalism. Consequently, the continuation of panics, depressions, and collapse can reasonably be expected to reoccur into the foreseeable future under a capitalist system. Either way, all this makes the need for structural change rather than a cycle of crisis–reform–crisis imperative.

A fourth rather dark possibility is that the emerging global elite have the ability and desire to consume at levels leading to market clearing or some sustainable level for a system to function. For example, Brazil and apartheid-era South Africa have (had) functioning economies based on an impoverished racial working class. Similarly, we may see a core-periphery divide not based primarily on geography or race but global class apartheid. Such a condition would lead to a revolutionary downgrading of working-class living standards in developed nations.

The alternative must be to create new economic models. But to create new models of production and consumption, one would have to alter the fundamental relations in both production and consumption so as to allow a mechanism through which global output can be consumed. How can these relations be altered to achieve market clearing? This is where libertarian socialist forms of societal organization have a solution: alter the relations of production through direct action to achieve self-organization, self-direction, and private productive property elimination, ushering in a new epoch versus a new capitalist stage.

Such a fundamental restructuring of national and global socioeconomic organization will not occur from impending collapse,[103] although I argue collapse is highly probable. The reason is that brutal oppressive regimes that are better armed than a national citizenry have proven capable of staying in power many years despite running their economies into grinding poverty, as demonstrated by many African dictatorships, such as Zimbabwe's. Therefore, direct action by a renewed transnational working-class movement will be required for fundamental structural changes.

This is also true given that countries such as China, whose own geoplitical and economic interests would be furthered by breaking off from the current US global regime, choose not to because in the short run it would plunge the Chinese and global economies into severe depression.[104] In turn, this would jeopardize the legitimacy of the elite's ruling status, possibly resulting in revolt. Thus, national elites and corporations in China and other nations may have no choice but to cooperate with the United States and invest their export earnings in the latter in order to support the existing system.[105] Therefore, it is not likely that a global downturn will be caused by power politics.

For these reasons a renewed labor movement will probably be fueled by delegitimization of the capitalist system.[106] This chapter has made the case that serious global crisis is still probable but accepts the argument of delegitimization. Rather, it is argued that the impetus for delegitimization will be the classic contradiction of overproduction and underconsumption.[107] This could lead to the renewed social movements predicted by a number of theorists.[108] However, it is hoped that such movements will be built in time to prevent the "Brazilification" of the developed world which some, including Barbara Ehrenreich, believe is already occurring in the United States. This is a pending new "Great Transformation" on capitalist terms, including a major degradation of living standards no less catastrophic than those discussed by Polanyi[109] and reiterated by Silver.[110] "A crisis of overproduction is likely to break out. ... the US economy's neoliberal structure may be reaching a limit in its ability to promote economic expansion and avert severe economic crises. ... If this occurs, the neoliberal institutional structure may not survive such a crisis."[111] According to Frank, "The historically necessary transition out from under the Uncle Sam run doughnut world could bring the entire world into the deepest depression ever."[112] If labor can obtain hegemony and accept the cataclysmic social changes ushered in by the forces of globalization based on human needs considerations instead, we could experience not a dystopia but a renewed golden age of social and scientific evolution resulting from a historic epochal change in the mode of production and consumption.

STRATEGIES OF RESISTANCE AND STRUCTURAL CHANGE

The labor movement may be weakened but it is never dead.[113] Today workers in developed nations, particularly the United States as the hegemonic power, must demand initial structural changes that can eventually evolve into deeper socioeconomic changes leading to a new global model and epochal change. Examples may include full-employment policies, universal health-care, guaranteed minimum living standards, fair trade, industrial democracy through works councils, repealing the corporate legal status of "person" for accountability, prohibiting all corporate involvement in the political process, and independence of the news media from corporate governance. Such demands can only be met by challenging the dominant ideology[114] with a radical *counter ideology*[115] (echoing Gramsci and Panitch and Gindin's call for delegitimization of capitalism); creating mass support and solidarity through *societal education*[116] along Gramscian and Freirean principles disseminated by worker-owned and-operated media; and engaging in *direct action* with civil disobedience, violent resistance, and even full-scale revolts. These strategies are based on an analysis of the US labor and civil rights history in chapter three, showing that this was how workers obtained most, if not all, their fundamental gains, like the eight-hour work-day. Such actions, though, would require a renewed and militant labor movement with an actual blueprint for an alternative form of socioeconomic organization or, as Gramsci called it, a *counter-hegemony*.[117]

To this end, unions need to continue expanding their focus beyond the shopfloor toward activism and global social justice, resisting existing legal, political, and economic structures instead of being co-opted.[118] Globally, workers of developed and developing nations have to further efforts to build a movement possibly based on the emerging strategies of transnational activism and Social Movement Unionism (SMU)[119] inclusive of gender, race, religion, culture, and geography.[120] In fact, the labor struggle has always been global, moving together with capital through global production sites and new product cycles.[121] The importance of SMU is that it can increase rank-and-file militancy in opposition to co-opted union bureaucracy.[122] Such renewed militancy will be pivotal in the fight for radical socioeconomic demands.

A classic example of a militant, sometimes revolutionary, union with a global outlook is the Industrial Workers of the World (IWW), affectionately known as the Wobblies, formed by socialists and anarchists. Other examples include transnational labor organizing by the International Trade Union Confederation, with over 300 affiliates representing 160 million workers in over 150 nations; Via Campesina, a transnational activist movement by rural women, landless peasants, small-to medium-scale farmers, and indigenous communities operating in the Americas,

Europe, Africa, and Asia; and the Transnationals Information Exchange (TIE) and the Canadian Auto Workers, both of which practice SMU.

However, SMU alone cannot succeed without the conscious choice to build and be part of broader revolutionary movements demanding fundamental restructuring in the relations of production.[123] This is why counter ideology and societal education are needed to offer a new model of society to be achieved with militant direct action fueled by global solidarity and independent worker institutions, e.g., media, schools, and activist political organizations. Although things are getting worse for the workers of the world, resistance is possible if it is based on the classic call for "workers of the world to unite" and challenge the legitimacy of the existing system. We need to reassert ourselves and not be intimidated into accepting an emperor with "new clothes" every time capitalism goes through a transformation. Once this is all said and done then we may see new direct actions that will usher in a long-overdue epochal change that will benefit humankind rather than the elite alone.

The next chapter of this book offers a closer look at counter ideology as the first step toward challenging the dominant ideology. It is through direct challenges to the dominant ideology, which legitimizes existing socioeconomic relations and shapes the political system, that fundamental change becomes possible. All other efforts, limited within the system's allowed parameters of discourse, are destined to failure as reformism. The capitalist system is designed to enrich the few by enslaving the many. Any efforts toward reforming this fundamental aspect of the system are stillborn since they leave the fundamental structure unchallenged. Change means challenging the structure which causes the undesirable outcomes; treating its symptoms is window dressing for the masses to create the illusion of democracy.

Notes

1. In economics, easy monetary policy increases the supply of money in the economy. A central monetary authority, such as the Federal Reserve System, seeks to make money plentiful in order to lower interest rates. The policy is used to spur growth, typically during recessions, by making it cheaper for businesses to borrow and invest. If implemented during times of economic growth it can lead to inflation, in this case of the housing market leading to the bubble that burst in 2007.
2. "Keynesian economics" refers to government interventions to regulate the economy. In recessions, tax cuts and or increased government spend-

ing are proposed to stimulate consumption. During peak output inflationary periods, tax increases and/or government spending cuts are suggested to cool down the economy.
3. Gordon, et al., 1982.
4. Kotz, et al., 1994.
5. In German *Produktionsverhältnisse*, the socioeconomic relationships in production corresponding to a particular epoch, e.g., the relationship between a capitalist and a worker in capitalism or master and slave in antiquity. According to Marx: "In the social production of their life, men enter into definite relations that are indispensable and independent of their will, relations of production appropriate which correspond to a definite stage of the development of their material productive forces. The sum total of these relations of production constitutes the economic structure of society, the real foundation, on which rises a legal and political superstructure and to which correspond definite forms of social consciousness." 1859 Preface to *A Contribution to the Critique of Political Economy*. Marx, 1978c: 4.
6. In German *Produktivkräfte*, the combination of the means of labor, e.g., tools, land, infrastructure with human labor power. It includes those forces which are applied by people in the production process. According to Marx, at some point of historical development, relations of production become outdated relative to the potential of productive forces effectively retarding the realization of their full potential: "At a certain stage of development, the material productive forces of society come into conflict with the existing relations of production, or – what is but a legal expression for the same thing – with the property relations within which they have been at work hitherto. From forms of development of the productive forces these relations turn into their fetters. Then begins an epoch of social revolution. With the changes of the economic foundation the entire immense superstructure is more or less rapidly transformed." 1859 Preface to *A Contribution to the Critique of Political Economy*. Marx, 1978c: 4–5.
7. Marx and Engels, 1978 [1848].
8. McDonough, 1994: 78.
9. From the Russian economist Nikolai Kondratiev (also written Kondratieff), long waves are cycles in the capitalist world economy averaging fifty and ranging from approximately forty to sixty years in length, consisting of alternating periods between high and relatively slow growth.
10. There is a distinction in Left literature often ignored between personal and productive private property. Personal private property is what the

individual owns as part of their daily life, e.g., a house, automobile, or television. Productive property is property used for economic activities earning income for the owners.

11. Physical, non-human inputs used in production such as factories, machines, and land used to produce wealth.

12. For example, in 2004 the top 1% of households owned 36.7% of all stock compared to 9.4% for the bottom 80% of households. Wolff, 2007.

13. Surplus value is a concept used by Karl Marx in his critique of political economy, although he did not himself invent the concept. It refers roughly to that part of the new value created by production which is claimed by enterprises as "generic gross profit." Marx argues that its ultimate source is unpaid surplus labor performed by the worker for the capitalist, and that the surplus value is the primary basis for capital accumulation. For Marx, the tremendous increase in wealth and population from the nineteenth century onward was mainly due to the competitive striving to obtain maximum surplus value from the employment of labor, resulting in an equally tremendous increase of productivity and capital resources.

14. Harvey, 2006.

15. In German, *Produktionsweise*, meaning "the way of producing," is a combination of productive forces and the means of production. "The mode of production of material life conditions the social, political and intellectual life process in general." 1859 Preface to *A Contribution to the Critique of Political Economy*. Marx, 1978c: 4–5. Once a mode of production is established it will re-create the forces and relations of production specific to it. Through historical development, a changing mode of production results in a new epoch according to Marx's historical materialism.

16. Wolfson, 2003.

17. O'Hara, 2001; Peck, 2002.

18. McMichael, 2008.

19. The concept of *globally segmented labor markets* was originally presented at the conference Growth and Crisis, Social Structure of Accumulation Theory and Analysis, National University of Ireland, Galway, Ireland, November 4, 2006. Session title: "Property and Its Limits." It was based on the extension of national regionally segmented labor markets developed by Gordon, Edwards, and Reich, 1982.

20. McMichael, 2008.

21. Under US hegemony, the Bretton Woods system of monetary management established the rules for commercial and financial relations

among the world's major industrial nations at the end of World War II. In July 1944, forty-four Allied nations gathered at the Mount Washington Hotel in Bretton Woods, New Hampshire, for the United Nations Monetary and Financial Conference. By 1945 Bretton Woods established the International Monetary Fund (IMF) and the International Bank for Reconstruction and Development (IBRD), commonly referred to as the World Bank. Chief features of the system were an obligation for each country to adopt a monetary policy that maintained the exchange rate of its currency within a fixed value—plus or minus 1%—in terms of gold and the ability of the IMF to bridge temporary imbalances of payments. On August 15, 1971, the Nixon administration unilaterally terminated convertibility of the dollar to gold, making the dollar the sole backing of currencies and a reserve currency for the member states. The action is also cited as the end of the Bretton Woods accord even though its main institutions continued to function.
22. IMF.
23. World Bank.
24. IMF.
25. World Bank.
26. Panitch and Gindin, 2005.
27. Ibid., 57.
28. McMichael, 2008.
29. Black, 2003.
30. Ibid.
31. US Census Bureau. Foreign Trade Statistics.
32. Black, 2003.
33. Zepezauer, 2004.
34. Panitch and Gindin, 2005: 47.
35. Frank, 2006: 30–31.
36. Scott, et al., 2006: 4.
37. Ibid.
38. Scott, 2007.
39. Ibid.
40. Ibid., 1.
41. Organisation for Economic Co-operation and Development, 2005: 36.
42. Ibid.
43. O'Hara, 2001.
44. McMichael, 2008; O'Hara, 2001.

45. Scott, et al., 2006: 2.
46. Gordon, et al., 1982.
47. Panitch and Gindin, 2005: 63–64
48. Cited in Peck, 2002: 212.
49. Fair trade is a social movement and market-based approach that aims to help producers in developing countries obtain better trading terms and promote sustainability. The movement advocates the payment of a higher price to producers as well as social and environmental standards. It focuses in particular on exports from developing countries to developed countries.
50. McMichael, 2008.
51. Dorgan, 2006; Peck, 2002; US Census Bureau, Historical Income Tables-Households.
52. Scott, 2007.
53. Dorgan, 2006.
54. National Labor Committee, various reports 2000–2006.
55. Banister, 2005.
56. US Department of Labor, Bureau of Labor Statistics, Division of International Labor Comparisons.
57. National Labor Committee, various reports 2000–2006.
58. Ibid.
59. Ibid.
60. Global Policy Forum, 2006.
61. Organisation for Economic Co-operation and Development, 2005: 12, 17, 46–47.
62. US Census Bureau. Foreign Trade Statistics.
63. Panitch and Gindin, 2005.
64. Frank, 2006.
65. Scott, 2007: 5.
66. The Gini coefficient was developed by the Italian statistician Corrado Gini and published in his 1912 paper "Variability and Mutability." It is commonly used as a measure of inequality of income or wealth. A value of 0 indicates total equality and a value of 1 maximal inequality.
67. US Census Bureau, Historical Income Tables-Households.
68. Fordism, named after Henry Ford, refers to various social theories about production and related socioeconomic organization. The essential meaning is that the worker must be paid higher wages in order to afford the products that the industrialist himself produces, causing an economy that runs full circle at optimum output.
69. O'Hara, 2004.

70. Ibid.
71. Kotz, 2006.
72. Ibid.
73. Ibid.
74. Marx, 1978b [1862–63]. Trickle-down economics, supply-side economics, and Say's Law refer essentially to the same concept. Namely, supply will create its own demand. However, the idea has been questioned since its origins and has not been proven to be true in light of recessions and depressions that according to the concept should not have occurred since supply creates its own demand.
75. Aronowitz, 2005.
76. Kotz, 2006.
77. Kotz, 2006; O'Hara, 2001, 2004.
78. The rate of exploitation is a concept in Marxian political economy. It refers to the ratio of the hours of necessary labor performed by workers and the hours of surplus labor worked by them. This is an economic relationship between quantities of hours worked, which is inferred from the amount of income workers actually get out of the total value of the output they produce. The rate of exploitation is often also equated with the rate of surplus value, but this is incorrect strictly speaking since the concept of the rate of exploitation can be applied to any type of class society in which workers perform surplus labor for their masters in any form.
79. Marx, 1978a [1867]; Marx, 1978b [1862–63].
80. McMichael, 2008: 1.
81. Frank, 2006.
82. Panitch and Gindin, 2005.
83. Productivity or an increase in efficiency is a measure of output from a production process, per unit of input. For example, labor productivity is typically measured as a ratio of output per labor-hour, an input. The common theory is that increases in productivity benefit both labor and capital assuming some equitable distribution. However, data has shown that productivity increases during the past few decades have almost exclusively been kept by capital, therefore also explaining stagnant real incomes.
84. Kotz, 2006; Leicht and Fitzgerald, 2007.
85. Frank, 2006; Kotz, 2006; Peck, 2002.
86. Kotz, 2006: 10.
87. Peck, 2002.
88. Leicht and Fitzgerald, 2007.

89. "The wealth effect" is an economic term referring to an increase in spending that accompanies an increase in perceived wealth. For example, if your stock or real estate investment rises threefold you will feel wealthier even though you do not actually possess that value as cash. This may also lead individuals to spend more than they normally would, given their income.
90. Kotz, 2006.
91. Leicht and Fitzgerald, 2007: 58.
92. Kotz, 2006.
93. Conkey, 2006; Leicht and Fitzgerald, 2007: 59, 93; Kotz, 2006: 11.
94. Panitch and Gindin, 2005: 66.
95. Peck, 2002: 180.
96. Marx, 1978a [1867], 1978b [1862–63].
97. As cited in Peck, 2002.
98. Frank, 2006; Peck, 2002; Kotz, 2006.
99. See, for example, Wolfson, 2003.
100. A reduction in earnings caused by a poor business climate, increased competition, or rising costs in this case increased labor costs. As a result, businesses may reduce output.
101. Ibid.
102. Panitch and Gindin, 2005.
103. Ibid
104. Frank, 2006.
105. Panitch and Gindin, 2005.
106. Ibid.
107. Moody, 1997.
108. See, for example, Clawson, 2003; Silver, 2003.
109. Polanyi, 2001 [1944].
110. Silver, 2003.
111. Kotz, 2006: 14.
112. Frank, 2006: 32.
113. Clawson, 2003; Moody, 1997; Silver, 2003.
114. The dominant ideology, in Marxist theory, is the set of common values and beliefs shared by most people in a given society, framing how the majority think about a range of topics. The dominant ideology reflects, or serves, the interests of the dominant class in that society. If the dominant ideology conflicted with the legitimacy of the dominant class's rule, then society would have to be in a state of war with itself, with the dominant class appearing as an illegitimate occupation. One way to understand Marxist revolutionary praxis is that it seeks to achieve just that

situation of social unrest in which the ruling class is seen as illegitimate—a necessary precursor to achieving the aim of overthrowing the dominant class of capitalism, the bourgeoisie. The ideology of the working class has to achieve dominance, in order for the working class to become the dominant class.

115. "Counter ideology," a term closely related to Antonio Gramsci, opposes the dominant ideology. Typically it is developed by opponents of the ruling elite to delegitimize their dominant ideology by exposing fallacies of the dominant ideology and offering better alternatives to how society should be organized, e.g., based on capitalist or communal principles.

116. "Education" as used in this book refers to the critical pedagogy developed by Paulo Freire and further developed by Giroux, McLaren, and others. See for example Giroux, 1988; McLaren and Leonard, 1992; McLaren, 2005.

117. "Counter-hegemony" refers to attempts to critique or dismantle hegemonic power. It is a confrontation and/or opposition to the status quo and its legitimacy in politics, but also other spheres of life, such as history, media, music, etc. If a counter-hegemony grows large enough it is able to subsume and replace the historic bloc it was born in. Neo-Gramscians use the Machiavellian terms "war of position" and "war of movement" to explain how this is possible. In a war of position a counter-hegemonic movement attempts, through persuasion or propaganda, to increase the number of people who share its view on the hegemonic order; in a war of movement the counter-hegemonic tendencies which have grown large enough overthrow, violently or democratically, the current hegemony and establish themselves as a new historic bloc.

118. Clawson, 2003; Moody, 1997; Park, 2007.

119. Social Movement Unionism attempts to integrate workers, trade unions and the labor movement into broader coalitions for social and economic justice. The campus living wage work of unions, which have frequently worked with chapters of United Students Against Sweatshops, are an example of the principle in practice.

120. Clawson, 2003;
121. Silver, 2003.
122. Moody, 1997.
123. Park, 2007.

2

Counter Ideology: Radical Evolutionary Change

> "At a certain stage of their development, the material productive forces of society come in conflict with the existing relations of production, or—what is but a legal expression of the same thing—with the property relations within which they have been at work hitherto. From forms of development of the productive forces these relations turn into their fetters. Then begins an epoch of social revolution."
>
> *Karl Marx*

IMAGINARY DEMOCRACY

If one argues that a radically different society based on egalitarian principles is possible, then it is necessary to directly confront the elite powerbrokers that dominate the political, social, and economic sectors of our society. This class-conscious elite controls the means of material production resulting in the following, according to Chomsky:

> All necessarily subordinate themselves and their interests to the overriding need to serve the needs of the owners and managers of the society, who, ... with their control over resources, are easily able to shape the ideological system (the media, schools, universities and so on) in their interests, to determine the basic conditions within which the political process will function, its parameters and basic agenda, and to call upon the resources of state violence, when need be, to suppress any challenge to entrenched power. The point was formulated ... by John Jay, the President of the Continental Congress and the first Chief Justice of the United States Supreme

Court: "The people who own the country ought to govern it." And, of course, they do, whatever political faction may be in power. Matters could hardly be otherwise when economic power is narrowly concentrated and ... basic ... investment decisions, ... are in principle removed from democratic control.[1]

Therefore, in addition to material resources, they also control ideological production through funding and staffing of think tanks, policy formation groups, and universities;[2] ownership of the mass media;[3] and domination of political institutions.[4] This effectively enables them to reproduce existing social relations domestically by preempting the emergence of counter ideologies and internationally, as outlined in chapter one, through globalization based on neoliberal policies imposed by the US state.[5]

Inside the Hegemonic State

That states represent the interests of their governing elites is not new. What is new, and deserving of analysis, is how this is done today and by whom. Specifically, US corporations have managed to construct neoliberal global regimes through control of domestic political, financial, and ideological institutions. These institutions are used to develop and promote a dominant ideology[6] that legitimizes capitalist relations in production and consumption domestically and abroad (Figure 2). First, the elite are conscious of their common interests making them a *class for themselves*,[7] whose interests are reflected in the composition of the boards of top financial institutions which form direct and indirect interlocks[8] with the boards of directors of major corporations.[9] This allows banks to function as coordinators and facilitators of capitalist interests.[10] For example, banks are the major stock voters in most top US corporations.[11] These nexuses reduce competition among companies by creating a common business agenda. Financial institutions also assist in formulating unified political agendas for corporations and the wealthy.[12] Thus, financial institutions function as ringleaders for forming a unified and highly conscious corporate-capitalist class.

Second, corporations have secured control of public policy formation by their de facto influence over major think tanks, foundations, universities,[13] and advisory groups through their deep and historical financial funding and staffing.[14] For example, the Council on Foreign Relations and the Conference Board are major policy formation groups with extensive ties to government and are mostly dominated by corporate executives and members of the upper class. Third, corporations corrupt the legislative process (the rule making) through lobbying, political contributions, political office staffing (despite clear conflicts of interest), and traditional forms of bribery.[15] In fact, the United States has obliterated the boundaries between business and politics, and between the public and private spheres. For example, corporate executives predominate in governmental positions that regulate their former employers. While former treasury secretary Henry Paulson was the CEO of Goldman Sachs, he requested the deregulations from the Securities and Exchange Commission (SEC) which caused the 2008 meltdown. He convinced the SEC to allow major financial institutions to increase their leverage and risk exposure by exempting them from the *net capital rule*[16] that required them to hold higher capital reserves. As treasury secretary, he then asked for the epic bailout of 2008, benefiting financial corporations, which were his true clients.

Former vice president Dick Cheney was the CEO of Halliburton, the company whose subsidiary won billions of dollars through no-bid contracts because of the war in Iraq—which he orchestrated through propaganda; former president George W. Bush is a former oil man who is tied to the medieval Saudi monarchy; New York City mayor Mike Bloomberg, who despite his earlier support for term limits ran for and won a third term, owns a media empire; former president Bill Clinton made millions in speaking fees after leaving office in addition to significant donations for his presidential library from governments and executives he met as president. The list goes on. What you will rarely find on any list of major political office holders is a person who has a high-school education or less making under $50,000 a year. This also happens to be the great majority of the population. Given the control of government by the wealthy and corporations, what we have is a plutocracy rather than democracy.[17]

Fourth, corporations control the flow of information and influence public perceptions by owning most means of disseminating information—the mass media.[18] Media concentration combined with corporate governance ensures the reproduction and reinforcement of the dominant ideology using advanced propaganda techniques while neutralizing critical dissent as exemplified by Rupert Murdoch's Fox network.[19] Having secured control over domestic policy formation and implementation, corporations are expanding neoliberalism globally through the US government, which effectively controls the rulemaking of the new regimes.[20] In short, there is no longer a debate of where power is centered, e.g., wealthy elite, corporations, or the state. Rather state power, capital, and the upper class have morphed into an interchangeable whole.

Figure 2. The Corporate Control Model

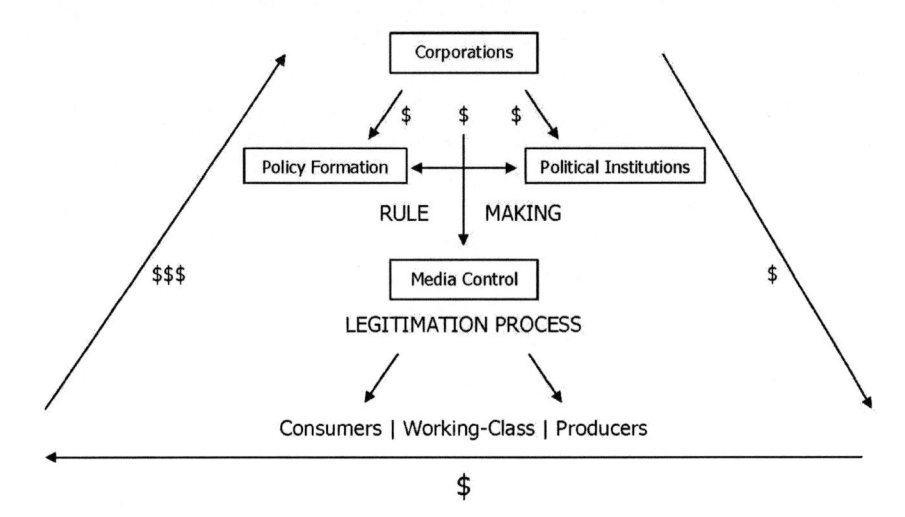

```
                        Corporations
                       ↙   $  $  $  ↘
            Policy Formation ←——→ Political Institutions
                          RULE | MAKING
                              ↓
      $$$              Media Control                    $
                     LEGITIMATION PROCESS
                       ↙           ↘
              Consumers | Working-Class | Producers
    ←─────────────────────────────────────────────────
                              $
```

In addition, elite ownership of the mass media inhibits the spread of counter ideologies. Rather, it promotes the reproduction of the dominant legitimizing myths by resocializing the perceptions of entire populations.[21] "In a well functioning state capitalist democracy like the United States, anything that might frighten the men of property is kept far from public eye."[22] Thus, more accurate and balanced reporting is supplanted by "news" heavily laced with a dogmatic agenda that supports the socioeconomic elite. For example, the Program on International Policy (PIPA)/Knowledge Networks Poll found Fox network viewers were far more likely to have inaccurate beliefs regarding basic facts related to economics, foreign policy, and so on, which reflected Republican propaganda aired on the network, and that, not surprisingly, they were more likely to support Bush administration policies.[23]

Continuation of such total domination of society is achieved in large part by controlling the educational system for the masses.[24] On the one hand, educational institutions—such as the corporate universities—are used as a tool of propaganda and indoctrination by the elite to reinforce their hegemonic culture.[25] As stated by Chomsky, "[the masses] are the

... targets of the mass media and a public education system geared to obedience and training in needed skills, including the skill of repeating patriotic slogans on timely occasions."[26] On the other hand, the quality of public education is attacked through unequal funding mechanisms, e.g., local property taxes for schools, resulting in inferior schooling for the poor and working class.[27] Access to affordable, quality higher education is also being limited through reduced state funding and rising tuition costs, thus putting higher education out of reach for working-class students.[28] The City University of New York, which was established primarily for the working class, did not charge tuition for over a century. Today it is mostly tuition-supported, limiting access to the underprivileged that it was created to serve.

Worse, what remains of critical thinking in the curriculum is systematically neutralized. This is achieved through the right-wing purges of "radical" faculty and attacks on free speech in general when the legitimacy of capitalism and its political structure are challenged.[29] Thus, we now have an educational system resembling a second-rate technical school. And, since the poor are more likely to oppose existing socioeconomic relations, limiting the quality or extent of their educational opportunities also limits the emergence of working-class intellectuals such as the author of this book—what Gramsci termed *organic intellectuals*[30]—who would be more likely to instigate radical ideological challenges.[31]

Consequently, fundamental social change can only occur through social movements promoting counter ideologies, challenging the legitimacy of the current dominant ideology that reinforces existing relations in production and consumption.[32] The threat of the power of divergent ideas is demonstrated by totalitarian regimes which censure the mass media while persecuting those who espouse non-sanctioned ideologies. Regimes like China's behave in this manner because, as Weber argues, when a system's legitimizing ideology or authority is undermined, it becomes unstable and prone to collapse.[33] We need look no further than the demise of the former Soviet Union to substantiate this.

Furthermore, for change to be lasting, the relations in production and consumption and so the mode of production itself, must be transformed. Anything short of a change in the mode of production would leave the fundamental system intact, exposing working-class gains to constant capitalist attacks.[34] This is demonstrated by the erosion of working-class gains in Western European economies as a result of globalization, the race to the bottom from competition with low-cost labor in developing nations, and a thoroughly disciplined American contingent workforce.

However, as Gramsci[35] noted, before advocating new societal arrangements, there would first have to be a demonstration of their superiority and feasibility relative to existing models. Here it is important to remember that capitalism, as with libertarian socialism, was not developed overnight by Adam Smith, nor did it take immediate political control of society. Instead, capitalism evolved over centuries and involved numerous hegemonic struggles between the aristocratic and bourgeois classes. Likewise, libertarian socialism's theoretical principles have been evolving for the past few centuries, but unlike capitalism it has had only sporadic real-world examples emerge at various times and places. Yet, in its limited actualization, libertarian socialism has been able to demonstrate the feasibility of the theory in practice as we will see shortly.

THEORETICAL ANALYSIS

As mentioned in the introduction, "working class" and "labor" are used interchangeably here and will refer to any person or household that does not own sufficient productive property to be able to live at an average lifestyle without being compelled to work. The libertarian socialist or anarchist principle of self-organization refers to a form of direct democracy—people representing themselves, while self-direction refers to worker owned and operated collective production.[36] Anarchism is one of the most diverse theoretical perspectives. It includes anarcho-communism, Marxism, syndicalism, participatory economics (parecon), mutualism, and much more, all of which are commonly referred to as libertarian socialism. As for the fundamental principles of anarchist forms of societal organization, Guerin, Rocker, and Ward provide an excellent review.[37] Kropotkin was one of the first to develop an anarcho-communist variant of anarchism.[38] To be clear, this author considers systems such as that of the former Soviet Union, China, and North Korea to be no more than brutal dictatorships. One concise description of the basic perspective of true libertarian socialism is as follows:

> Libertarian socialism ... is a group of political philosophies that aspire to create a society without political, economic, or social hierarchies, i.e. a society in which all violent or coercive institutions would be dissolved, and in their place every person would have free, equal access to the tools of information and production.

This equality and freedom would be achieved through the abolition of authoritarian institutions that own and control productive means as private property, so that direct control of these means of production and resources will be shared by society as a whole. Libertarian socialism also constitutes a tendency of thought that informs the identification, criticism and practical dismantling of illegitimate authority in all aspects of social life.

Libertarian socialists place their hopes in trade unions, workers' councils, municipalities, citizens' assemblies, and other non-bureaucratic, decentralized means of direct democracy. Many libertarian socialists advocate doing away with the state altogether, seeing it as a bulwark of capitalist class rule, while others propose that a minimal, non-hierarchical version is unobjectionable.[39]

A key goal of libertarian socialists is the elimination of all forms of government in favor of self-organization, based on the argument that any government by definition results in the suppression of the many by the few. This is held to be true of democracies, as well, in that they are also dominated by elites and therefore will not benefit the working class.[40] Democracies are acknowledged to provide some benefits as a result of working-class participation but these are seen as minor and perpetually under attack by elite interests.[41] According to Rocker, one of the most articulate exponents of anarchist theory:

The peoples owe all the political rights and privileges . . . not to the good will of their governments, but to their own strength. Governments have employed every means that lay in their power to prevent the attainment of these rights or to render them illusory. Great mass movements among the people and whole revolutions have been necessary to wrest these rights from the ruling classes, who would never have consented to them voluntarily. . . . Only after the workers had by direct action confronted parliament with accomplished facts, did the government see itself obliged to take the new situation into account and give legal sanction to the trade unions. *What is important is not that governments have decided to concede certain rights to the people, but the reason why they have had to do this.*[42]

This is supported by data indicating a long-term trend from 1970 in declining real wages and benefits due to the rise of and attacks by neoliberal ideologies including all US administrations.[43] Chapter three shows how it was through direct action that labor and civil rights movements extracted meaningful concessions from the power elite. This is why anarchism stresses direct action not only to obtain but also preserve gains. According to Rocker:

> Political rights do not originate in parliaments, they are . . . forced upon parliaments from without. . . . even their enactment into law has for a long time been no guarantee of their security. Just as the employers always try to nullify every concession they had made to labour as soon as opportunity offered, as soon as any signs of weakness were observable in the workers' organisations, so governments also are always inclined to restrict or to abrogate completely rights and freedoms that have been achieved if they imagine that the people will put up no resistance. . . . Political rights do not exist because they have been legally set down on a piece of paper, but only when they have become the ingrown habit of a people, and when any attempt to impair them will meet with the violent resistance of the populace.[44]

More so, for fundamental changes benefiting the working class to be lasting, anarchists argue that direct action would have to be revolutionary, leading to new radical forms of societal organization based on the principles of self-organization in civil society and self-direction in production. However, such societal change can be both revolutionary and evolutionary as will be shown shortly.

Conditions for Capitalist Growth

Ideology and political institutions shape class conflict and thus the relations in production and consumption.[45] The outcome of class conflict and the resulting shape of class relations determine the creation of new economic, political, cultural, and ideological institutional structures referred to as Social Structures of Accumulation (SSA) that determine the distribution of expansionary gains, as well. However, the SSAs will be conducive to future expansion and accumulation, depending on the capitalists' willingness to invest according to external institutional arrangements.

This institutional approach to capitalist expansion underscores the classic Marxist critique of overproduction and underconsumption, and capitalism's inherent contradictions.[46] More so, stagnation results when either capital or labor dominates the other.[47] As Table 4 shows, in free market periods capital dominates labor, leading to contraction caused by underconsumption; but when labor dominates capital, it leads to contraction due to a profit squeeze.

Table 4. Power, Contraction, and Expansion

Dominant capital period	↑π↓W↓C↑Q contraction due to underconsumption
Dominant labor period	↑W↑C↓π↓Q contraction due to profit squeeze
Capital balanced with labor	↑W↑C↑Q↑π economic expansion

Whereas π is corporate profits, W is wages, C is consumption, and Q is output.

Accordingly, periods of expansion are based on SSAs that regulate class conflict, leading to a balance of power between capital and labor. This can be expressed roughly as profit and wage considerations being balanced—leading to a level of purchasing power, consumption, and aggregate demand capable of clearing output. However, historical contingencies would make it difficult to sustain such a balance of power between capital and labor, which would lead to long periods of expansion under stable SSAs and contraction when they crumble. Ultimately, all SSAs, regardless of the power arrangements, will be destabilized because these are based on a capitalist mode of production. As such, capital inevitably obtains the upper hand relative to labor:

> Capitalists have a decided advantage in a capitalist economy: they own the capital. As a result, they also have more income and wealth. They can use their privileged position to influence the state to their advantage, both when they share power with labor and when they dominate labor.[48]

This triggers a reaction from labor, leading to the ongoing dialectical succession of emerging and declining SSAs, depending on which class dominates at a given historical moment.

The argument of a profit squeeze underscores another important fact. Even if labor obtains an upper hand through revitalized movements and pro-labor government policies, it still would not provide a lasting solution.[49] As long as the relations of production remain capitalist, there can only be a temporary illusion of prosperity and ephemeral gains for the working class because a period of dominant labor would inevitably result in a profit squeeze which would trigger a recession and a realignment of class power anew. Cyclical downturns caused by either insufficient purchasing power or a profit squeeze are integral to the capitalist system, and the true cause of business cycles and Kondratieff long waves. Take, for instance, where the line of class conflict lies in Figure 3. When ownership of the means of production is private, an increase in the public proportion of total societal wealth reduces profits, as a result of which capitalists limit production. An increase in the private proportion results in reduced overall purchasing power.

In contrast, libertarian socialist principles of societal organization resolve the problems of overproduction and underconsumption and a profit squeeze. The real problem is private productive property, a long-held position of anarchists and Marxists:

> At a certain stage of their development, the material productive forces of society come in conflict with the existing relations of production, or—what is but a legal expression of the same thing—with the property relations within which they have been at work hitherto. From forms of development of the productive forces these relations turn into their fetters. Then begins an epoch of social revolution.[50]

If, for example, private ownership of the means of production is replaced by communal ownership, profit considerations are eliminated from the production decisions. Thus, there could be a situation where $W = C = Q$ = market clearing, whereas W is wages, C is consumption, and Q is output. This is because under libertarian socialist societal organization the worker is also the owner (self-direction). Since all workers would also be owners, it is reasonable to argue that all net profits, or the majority of them, would be paid out to the workers either as wages or profits which would become synonymous. This creates a far broader distribution of wealth and consequent purchasing power and aggregate demand, leading to market clearing by eliminating the conflict between profits and wages or capital and labor. This is in contrast to capitalism, where profits are concentrated in the hands of a few whose demand is insufficient to clear markets and who are likely to invest in either low-wage or non–job generating sectors.[51] Thus, the capitalists have replaced the aristocracy in terms of who determines how societal resources are managed and distributed. Libertarian socialism replaces individual control with societal control over resources.

What Is Wealth?

Proudhon famously asked *"What Is Property?"* in his book by the same title, answering that "property is theft." Accordingly, today we can state that private wealth is a fiction. Rather, "wealth" is a euphemism for stolen resources from the commons. Looking at Figure 3 we see what many anarchists, Marxists, and progressive intellectuals have argued for centuries. Namely, there is only societal wealth. This is the sum of a society's total wealth. It includes the zeitgeist of the epoch, its mode, means, relations, and forces of production, overall levels of knowledge and discovery, and natural resources including land, air, and sea. Henry Ford, Bill Gates, and all other capitalists did not invent, create, or innovate anything. They simply built on the overall publicly available social level of development—the existing knowledge base. Their only innovation was how to usurp from the pot of social wealth.

Looking at Figure 3, societal wealth is finite at a given time although over time it can expand or contract, just like a nation's GDP. If one accepts that wealth thus defined is social, then private wealth is but the removal of wealth from the overall stock. The divide between public and private is therefore socially constructed by conmen called entrepreneurs today, feudal lords and kings in other times. The dividing line in the figure represents class conflict. When the upper-class thieves dominate, the line is pushed into the public domain, increasing the share of the privately controlled wealth, and vice versa. Government, corporations, the media, education, guns, and tanks are all weapons used in this class warfare by the various social groups to move the line in their advantage. Consequently, by definition class war is a zero sum game at a given time. An increase in one side of the sphere can only come at the expense of the other.

This is what is meant by privatization under capitalist globalization: the proportion of social wealth being siphoned through legal fictions from the public commons. Alternatively, class conflict determines the flow of wealth between the public and private spheres. This struggle has been demonstrated in every epoch. During feudalism, it was the aristocracy that managed to secure large societal resources as with the infamous English enclosure laws of the twelfth, eighteenth, and nineteenth centuries at the expense of peasants. Remember the little boy's crime according to the Sheriff of Nottingham when Robin Hood was returning home? He was poaching in the "king's forest." Then came the bourgeois revolutions after which I am the trespasser on Bill Gate's company grounds or use "*his* stolen software" without paying him. The time has come for us to declare that all capitalists are trespassing on our public wealth, our commons, to which they too would be given access as citizens, to push the class conflict line back until our commons are whole again. This also implies another revolutionary idea: the elimination of all copyrights and patents, returning knowledge to the public domain. After all, most basic and theoretical research is publically funded through university labs, government grants, the military, etc. Yet, the applications of that basic research are given patents, typically to corporations. Innovation therefore occurs at public expense while the benefit is privatized.

Figure 3. Total Societal Wealth

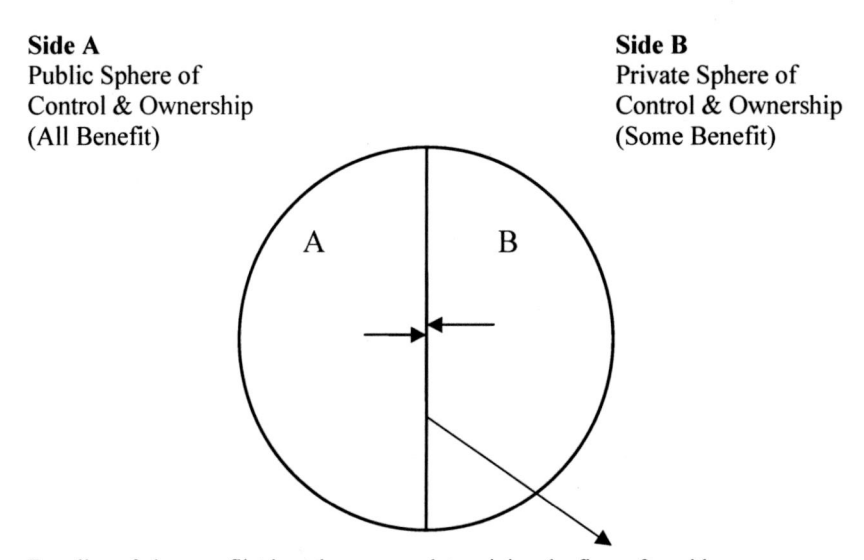

Side A
Public Sphere of
Control & Ownership
(All Benefit)

Side B
Private Sphere of
Control & Ownership
(Some Benefit)

Frontline of class conflict based on power determining the flow of wealth

Similarly, real growth, such as that measured by GDP, is not material. Rather, the only form of true growth is knowledge. It is knowledge that allows people to create what we see around us. For example, the material building blocks for everything from skyscrapers and computers to spaceships have always been present. What was lacking was the knowledge of how to combine things to create what we have today. Therefore, a society's overall level of knowledge is the only measure of not just growth but real value as well. In addition, a society's pool of knowledge increases positively with the extent of societal education because we are all capable of intellectual production and more educated minds can result in more discoveries and inventions.[52] This also includes access to knowledge which is limited by copyrights and patents. Since everything is a product of accumulated societal knowledge, so too discoveries and inventions are socially produced even if it was an individual that put two and two together. Copyrights and patents are private property rights and as such remove knowledge from society's overall pool. This means less people have access to knowledge hidden behind patents and thus innovation is delayed. In short, patents and copyrights are the equivalent of privatizing knowledge and therefore true value and wealth.

Revolutionary Action and the Relations of Production

According to Marxist economism, new relations depend on the full development of productive forces. Anarchist theory holds that even fully developed forces of production are no guarantee that capitalism will collapse under the weight of the contradiction between the new forces and the old relations. This has been demonstrated by capitalism's continual transformations made possible by the use of force by the governing elite regardless of the delivery mechanism such as the state. Ironically, in order to explain the lack of capitalism's inevitable fall, Marxists have developed a dependency on class consciousness[53] and ideology in general as a precondition for working-class action. Therefore, it is the relations of production that shape the mode of production while the mode of production determines the mode of distribution and thus consumption.[54]

The forces of production are, in and of themselves, unrelated to distribution, which is determined by the relations of production. Moreover, the relations of production are also relations in consumption. It is within both spheres that dominant ideological structures of legitimization are constructed and promoted through political and cultural institutions like the media. Therefore, economics and ideology interact to form a given mode of production and distribution. Once a mode of production is established, the forces of production reproduced within it do not necessarily remain unchanged, but can be altered as through scientific discovery. Similarly, a mode of production reproduces the relations of production which do not necessarily remain unchanged, but can be altered as through education. Therefore, the relations of production can be altered by chance or evolution but also deliberate human agency such as direct action[55] fueled by the ideological delegitimization of society's production-consumption structures in industry and politics.[56] Since the relations of production are a determinant of the mode, altering the former can alter the latter and in turn the mode of distribution and consumption. Therefore, it is changes in the relations of production that alter the system, causing it to evolve into a different epoch in t_2 (Figure 4).

Figure 4. Dialectical Change and Libertarian Socialism

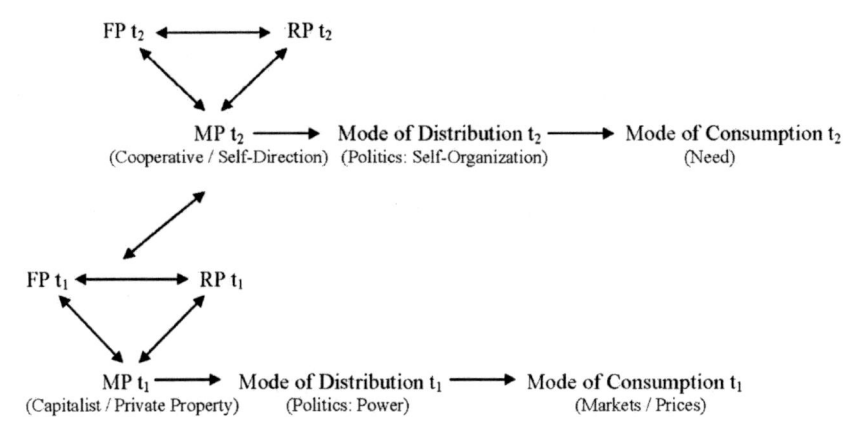

```
        FP t₂ ←――――→ RP t₂
              ↘   ↙
               ↘ ↙
            MP t₂ ――――→ Mode of Distribution t₂ ――――→ Mode of Consumption t₂
    (Cooperative / Self-Direction)   (Politics: Self-Organization)        (Need)
               ↗
              ↗
        FP t₁ ←――――→ RP t₁
              ↘   ↙
               ↘ ↙
            MP t₁ ――――→ Mode of Distribution t₁ ――――→ Mode of Consumption t₁
    (Capitalist / Private Property)    (Politics: Power)              (Markets / Prices)
```

Mode of Production (MP); Relations of Production (RP); Forces of Production (FP)

Furthermore, as many have argued, it is ideology which shapes the material world.[57] Specifically, it is the overall pool of knowledge combined with the extent of educational attainment within a society which generate ideology and develop the material forces of production. The greater the educational level of a population, the more knowledge that can be applied to the forces of production, e.g., more productive machines and software. But, the more extensive education is, the more the possibility of reaching underprivileged social subgroups. However, if a society has subordinate groups it must control them physically, often with violence but primarily with internalized control via a legitimizing ideology usually embedded in superstition, such as religion. The Hindu religion with its caste system is a classic example. Education has the effect of increasing self consciousness and the ability to articulate and reflect upon unequal relations.[58] As such, although a society's productive forces are developed further when education is widespread, it also gives birth to a class-conscious counter ideology by subordinate groups. From that point, it is only a matter of time before the subordinate group demands new relations in production and society in general. This is the true birth of revolution. The spread of knowledge through critical education develops the productive forces *and* gives birth to ideological challenges to the old relations.

Interestingly, a libertarian socialist society is neither utopian nor dependant on the forces of production. It has been the basis of societal organization, in one form or another, both spontaneously and planned throughout history. "An Anarchist society, a society which organizes itself without authority, is always in existence ... far from being a speculative vision of a future society, it is a description of a mode of human organization, rooted in the experience of everyday life, which operates side by side with, and in spite of, the dominant authoritarian trends of our society."[59] Multiple examples of anarchy in practice include the old US labor movement,[60] such as the Seattle general strike of 1919; the Paris Commune of 1871 and 1968; the early Soviets in Russia, 1917; Kronstadt 1917; Makhnovtchina and Ukraine 1919–1921; post-1919 Italy; and the Spanish Revolution in Catalonia, 1936–1939. It is generally accepted that these ultimately failed due to overwhelming reactionary state force, internal sabotage and betrayal, and timing.

Timing is of particular importance but in contrast to Marxist economism, anarchist theory implies that the relations of production need a level of development for new forms of societal organization to be lasting. For example, Gramsci argues through his theory of hegemony that a precondition for socialism includes the ideological development of a feasible alternative or counter-hegemony to existing forms of societal organization.[61] This would be accomplished through the objective societal education of the working class, combined with experience functioning within alternative forms of organization. Rocker also emphasized worker education as a precondition for action.[62] In addition, Bakunin, Malatesta, and Proudhon[63] concluded that the anarchist experiments of their time ultimately failed because workers lacked the education and overall experience with these new societal forms of organization rather than due to inherent systemic flaws of anarchism.

Evolutionary Radical Societal Transformation

In order to obtain lasting fundamental changes benefiting the working class, anarchists and many Marxists argue direct action would have to be revolutionary, leading to new radical forms of societal organization based on the principles of self-organization in civil society and self-direction in production. Such societal change can be both revolutionary and evolutionary. One way of measuring societal change is by the extent to which personnel in positions of domination are exchanged.[64] This results in a continuum of structural change ranging from total change of personnel (sudden) to no exchange (evolutionary change). However, sudden change is not necessarily radical but radical change can be sudden or evolutionary. Thus "revolutionary change" could refer to and is used interchangeably in the literature to describe both sudden and radical change. What then determines sudden versus radical change? Radical change is positively correlated with the intensity of class conflict, whereas sudden change is positively correlated with the level of violence:

> ... intensity refers to the energy expenditure and degree of involvement of conflicting parties. A particular conflict may be said to be of high intensity if the cost of victory or defeat is high for the parties concerned. . . . The violence of conflict relates rather to its manifestations than to its causes; it is a matter of the weapons that are chosen by conflict groups to express their hostilities. Again, a continuum can be constructed ranging from peaceful discussions to militant struggles such as strikes and civil wars. . . . The scale of degree of violence, including discussion and debate, contest and competition, struggle and war, displays its own patterns and regularities. Violent class struggles, or class wars, are but one point on this scale.[65]

Although sudden and radical change can occur together, as with high levels of violence and intensity, these concepts could also be mutually exclusive. This book argues in favor of evolutionary radical change to prevent the rise of unforeseen new totalitarian regimes as with the Bolsheviks. As important, an overnight abolition of government or private productive property would result in various immediate dislocations. Specifically, sudden and spontaneous revolutions often lack organization and leadership, resulting in ephemeral riots, random violence, or chaos. What is more, societal dislocations of catastrophic proportions have been the outcome of sudden radical change as with the sudden shift in the 1990s of the Soviet Union toward free markets, a shift that devastated an entire generation while giving birth to a new dominant class, the *oligarchs*. According to Polanyi, the same catastrophic impact was experienced in England when capitalism asserted total control over society within one generation.[66]

Moreover, even a revolution with strong leadership is doomed to fail. According to anarchist theory, any elite group, including intellectuals, ultimately will impose its own agenda at the expense of the many. This led Bakunin to predict the rise of Bolshevik totalitarianism. According to Bakunin, the intellectual elites "will seek to assume the reins of state power ... exploiting popular struggles for their own ends, and in the name of 'science' and their alleged superior understanding will drive the 'ignorant masses' to a form of 'socialism' that will 'serve to conceal the domination of the masses by a handful of privileged elite.'"[67] In other words, every form of government is a form of control. Ironically, this view is shared by extremist capitalists, the libertarians. As such, any true and meaningful change to obtain an egalitarian society must be led by the masses themselves. Marxists argue that people need to achieve class consciousness in order to engage in class action led by the intellectuals. Similarly, anarchists also believe it is the people themselves that need to act rather than to be led by elites—intellectuals included.

In addition, history shows that people themselves fail to make new forms of societal organization achieve lasting power during sudden radical change. Many theorists and revolutionaries have concluded that a major reason is the lack of experience and education of the working class with these alternative forms of societal organization.[68] For example, Proudhon thought that the revolution of 1848 could not bring full anarchism because it occurred prematurely relative to the level of development in the relations of production:

> Proudhon, in the midst of the 1848 Revolution, wisely thought that it would be asking too much of his artisans to go, immediately, all the way to "anarchy." In default of this maximum program, he sketched out a minimum libertarian program: progressive reduction in the power of the State, parallel development of the power of the people from below, through what he called clubs, and which the man of the twentieth century would call councils.[69]

Additionally, for the masses to engage in a decentralized functional revolution without elite leadership requires societal education to obtain a level of class consciousness and understanding that would not require the reproduction of an authoritarian social structure. Thus, the paradox for anarchists that Proudhon and later Gramsci[70] realized: to eventually obtain a communal society, one must tolerate the state until there is a sufficient base developed among the population that can understand and function within an alternative socioeconomic framework.

Therefore, it is transformative critical education that will ultimately spark action and change.[71] Such change must be evolutionary by a process of direct action challenging key elements of existing relations in production and consumption. This does not mean that such change cannot be highly revolutionary and radical,[72] because changing the relations of production makes it possible to alter the mode of production and thus the relations in production and consumption (distribution). This is why national elites through their control of the state always attempt to control the media, while curtailing critical education.[73] This is true of dictatorships like China with overt control and censorship and true of Western democracies like the United States with covert control and censorship, via a more advanced and sophisticated concentration of media ownership and corporate governance.[74]

In sum, ideology, critical education, and action are the basic engines of social change. When a counter ideology is born out of historical conditions or necessities, it articulates an antithesis. This is an antithesis to the existing material and ideological social structures, or the base and superstructures in Marxist terms. This, rather than new forces of production, is the birth of revolutionary social conflict, for two different visions of social organization are locked into a hegemonic struggle. Societal education is the battlefield in the minds of a population over which the hegemonic conflict plays out. The mass media, schools, and culture as through art, are the tools through which societal education becomes possible. Education by groups espousing the counter ideology can increase the intensity of class conflict, making it more radical, if it can reach the masses.[75] Action which is encouraged by a counter ideology, disseminated among the public through critical education, can range from silent disagreement to violent revolution. The combination of revolutionary action and intense class conflict can result in sudden social change that is also radical or transformative. However, radical transformative change can also be evolutionary in that it does not have to occur within a day or year.

The Radical Seed for New Relations of Production

To obtain egalitarianism, the working class does not need to end or overthrow governments that generally respect civil rights. Instead, it could engage in militant direct action combined with defensive violence for strategic demands that challenge existing relations in production, laying the foundations for fundamental and lasting evolutionary change. But what would be an example of such a demand? Capital, government, and the elite have morphed into an indistinguishable whole, as has been argued. They have created a holistic unified system of domination, a new zeitgeist of capitalist aristocracy, with the corporation as its center of gravity. From the corporate control model (Figure 2) we see how it is capital that dictates government and policy making (legislative process), ideological production (educational institutions and think tanks),[76] and media (means of dissemination and legitimization). In short, corporate domination of government has replaced the state as the power base of societal control, or more accurately the two have merged, with the former in the driver's seat. Therefore, to paraphrase Marx and Lenin, it is control of the corporation as the economic base of capitalist power that workers should target to obtain control over production-consumption arrangements, including the state, in the process.

Practically speaking, this translates into control of corporate policy-making through corporate boards of directors and executives. By totally replacing personnel in *these* positions of domination via militant direct action, sudden revolutionary change becomes possible while avoiding the total destruction of existing institutional arrangements. The working class can demand that each corporate board of directors, say of the Fortune 2000, be comprised exclusively by workers of the enterprise and community representatives, while leaving stock ownership private. This is synonymous with ending "private control" of private productive property and establishing private ownership, but with "public governance." More to the point, half the board could be composed of employees elected by the company's workers. They should be recallable any time, for any reason, by initiatives and a simple majority vote. The other half would be community representatives from grassroots and nonprofit organizations, e.g., Food Not Bombs, American Association of University Professors, etc. Organizations affiliated, representing, or serving as fronts for capital and the elite must be excluded, e.g., the Conference Board, the Business Roundtable, the Business Council, American Enterprise Institute, Council on Foreign Relations, Hudson Institute, etc. These community representatives should also be elected, from the membership of their organizations, and be recallable any time for any reason.

The new boards would have the power to nominate all the "chiefs" and top executives, e.g., CEOs, CFOs, presidents, etc. These officers could also be nominated by workers and ballot write-ins. However, once nominated they would have to receive confirmation by a simple majority vote from the employees. Furthermore, these officers could be removed any time, for any reason, either by the board or recall vote by the employees that would override any board decision. In fact, any majority vote by the workers would override the board in matters of company operations. Of course, all this leaves many details to be considered because it is up to the workers and community to decide those, giving the new system flexibility. And by the way, do you think any worker would vote for a CEO to earn tens of millions even as the company is run into the ground, only to "parachute" out with even more millions?

This proposal is the logical evolution of the anarcho-communist concept of self-management[77] and Bakunin's federated communes that would be the basis of self-rule. Such communes would then evolve into labor councils[78] to replace government. Although much of this has not occurred on any long-term basis, the related anarcho-syndicalist concept of works councils has become a reality in some industrialized nations.

Germany and France offer good examples of how works councils operate. First, council members are elected by their coworkers. These works councils are mandated by law for firms of a certain size, but they are not unions, although in southern Europe they may act as such. This means the councils cannot negotiate over wage issues, as in northern Europe, and are often required by law to cooperate with employers.[79]

An important difference between national works councils is whether they are given codetermination in addition to rights of consultation and information. When only consultation and information rights are provided, the councils still have a high degree of power within the production process that greatly empowers workers, as is clearly demonstrated below:

> Works councils laws invariably obligate employers to disclose to the council information about major new investment plans, acquisition and product market strategies, planned reorganization of production, use of technology, and so on. And council laws typically require employers to consult with the council on workplace and personnel issues, such as work reorganization, new technology acquisition, reductions or accretions to the work force, transfers of work, over-time, and health and safety.[80]

However, when works councils are given codetermination they become even more powerful labor institutions because codetermination requires that employers obtain approval for certain decisions from the councils. Should a council refuse to approve a managerial decision, it can mount legal action and challenge the employer. Therefore, the laws provide resolution mechanisms such as arbitration, grievance committees, and special labor courts. Germany is an excellent example of a country with works councils enjoying codetermination rights:

> German works councils enjoy information rights on financial matters ... In addition, however, they have codetermination rights on such matters as principles of remuneration, introduction of new payment methods, fixing of job and bonus rates and performance-related pay, allocation of working hours, regulation of overtime and short-time working, leave arrangements, vacation plans, suggestion schemes, and the introduction and use of technical devices to monitor employees' performance. They also enjoy prescribed codetermination rights on individual staff movements, including hiring, evaluation, redeployment, and dismissal, and the right to a "reconciliation of interests" between the council and the employer on a wide range of other matters bearing on the operation of the firm.[81]

When talking about "reconciliation of interests" it is important to note that this means workers also have power over what is produced, as well as any closures and relocations in parts or all of the company plant. Consequently, codetermination indicates extensive workers' power in its active institutional form. Even in the absence of codetermination, works councils in and of themselves are indicative of higher levels of institutionalized workers' power, given their right to access company information. This is the case with France's works councils which are given rights to information and consultation, but not codetermination.

The societal control of corporate boards represents the next evolutionary step from works councils toward libertarian socialist societal organization with an intermediary compromise to the abolition of private productive property. Such a fundamental change in class power relations will alter corporate behavior to reflect the public good and eliminate production externalities[82] and corporate free-rider[83] problems. Communities could prohibit the use of corporate wealth and ownership to influence the political process or the news media. The managerial class of capitalist private property could be instructed to operate under new parameters of production, using sustainable technology, offering all employees substantive benefits, living wages, and reasonable workloads. Furthermore, this would also eliminate the most common excuse that corporations offer for not being socially responsible: "we will not be competitive if we employ these practices, because our competitors do not." If the community has the final say on all boards, it is reasonable to argue that a consensus of demands will arise with high corporate responsibility, which will level the cost playing field for companies. This form of evolutionary revolution is very radical in that the authority of private productive property over society would be seriously limited if not eliminated altogether. Yet, this would provide fundamental changes that do not require the immediate destruction of basic societal institutions.

Furthermore, what is suggested would lay the Gramscian foundation for a true libertarian socialist epoch via a combination of direct action and democracy to achieve the ending of corporate rule over the media, politics, and production. Also, worker and community governance of corporations could evolve into a groundbreaking real-life experimental school for the practice of self-direction and organization.[84] This would demonstrate to workers that they themselves are capable of self-directed production without elite corporate owners.[85] Subsequently, the citizenry's realization that since the majority of stocks are owned by the elite few, ending private productive property would be in the interest of society at large. It may only take a public awareness of the fact that the top 1% of US households received 34.8% of the stock market gains of 1989–1998, while the richest 10% received 72.5%, and the bottom 80% received only 13.6%.[86] Looking at Table 5 it becomes clearer just how concentrated ownership of productive property is in the United States. Combined with the lessons in transformative education and self-direction, this would provide the impetus for self-rule.

Table 5. Wealth Distribution in 2001

Percent of:	Bottom 90%	Top 10%	Top 1%
Total Net Worth	15.5*	84.4**	33.4
Ownership of All Stocks	15.5*	89.3**	33.5
Pension Accounts	39.6	60.3	13.3
Business Equity	10.4	89.6	57.3
Debt	74.1	25.9	5.8

Source: Domhoff, http://whorulesamerica.net/power/wealth.html
*Bottom 80%
**Top 20%

Ideally, as the public better comprehends that control of the economic base of society can result in working-class goals through control of productive property, government as we know it will be rendered unnecessary. Thus, new direct action to end government would be in a stronger position once the economic base of society is seized and relations of production have evolved. Its replacement could be the fruit of the radical seed of human social evolution: an administrative system such as Bakunin's federated communes based on anarcho-communist principles including self-rule and self-direction. Mechanisms, such as those discussed by Proudhon,[87] could also be put into place to guard against the emergence of authoritarianism. For example, one-year service limits on governing bodies combined with the ancient Greek concept of filling public office by lottery, could produce a more advanced political system less vulnerable to large-scale corruption than many in existence today.

New Evolutionary Relations of Consumption

New productive relations would also require new relations in consumption. Namely, a socioeconomic system must address not only how to produce, whether under self-management or not, but also how to distribute products and services, whether based on a wage system or not. There is virtual agreement among Marxist and progressive scholars regarding the shortcomings of distribution based on a wage-based market system. Interestingly, whenever self-management was actually practiced in the form of works councils or community councils, as in Spain, 1936, one of the main problems was to figure out how one pay in and receive from the community resources—distribution, in other words.[88] Practically this meant counting hours worked as payment into the system for "community credits" with which to "purchase" supplies at the community "store." This was the practical solution to problems with more idealistic libertarian socialist formulas of exchange mechanisms that would try to implement the slogan "to each according to need, from each according to ability." Unfortunately, such a simple idea turned out to be very difficult to put in practice. How can community governance be combined with an economic system that is egalitarian *and* fair? Namely, how do we count?

Many anarchists and Marxists are not economists and tend to associate words like "price" and "wage" with all that is wrong with society. The problem, though, is not the concept of price or wage. Rather, the problem is what determines them and how they are defined. More to the point, prices and wages serve the basic function of rationing or distribution.[89]

The real problem is that wage levels are set by class power relations that determine in turn which skill sets (labor) are valued. This type of value is therefore fictitious. It creates a stratification of labor from the undervalued to the overvalued. Consequently, wages are a form of rationing based on class power instead of an objective measure of time worked. For example, many studies have found the exorbitant compensation of top CEOs in America cannot be justified by their market performance but by class power relations.[90] In any case, every society needs prices and wages or, stated differently, a system of distribution. However, what distribution and thus prices and wages represent can vary significantly. Communal economies can still have prices and wages for their rationing and guiding functions but change the basis upon which these are set. In addition, combined with worker-citizen participatory empowerment through self-direction and organization, people would feel like true stakeholders, making this system more productive.

First, if we accept that all people are equal, then all socially necessary labor is also equal. If society should not be stratified, then neither should labor. This makes socially necessary "labor" a homogeneous concept or "product" measured by standard units of time at a given social average of intensity and ability. Just like a gallon of milk is the same regardless of who produced it, one hour's worth of street cleaning is equal to one hour worked by a medical doctor. Why? Because all socially necessary labor is, well, labor. What Marx saw as complex or compound labor (versus average or simple labor) was instead knowledge. It is a society's pool of accumulated knowledge which builds on past discoveries that can be compound or complex. Labor is the *medium* through which knowledge is applied to the physical world in order to alter it. As such, all socially necessary labor, mental and physical, is equal—irrespective of who or what performs the work or is more adept at this or that task—to be measured by standard units of time, e.g., one hour's worth of work. Let's not confuse wages or market supply and demand, which are determined by class power, in terms of which labor is valued, for actual value. There is a difference between a wage and labor. Wages are unequal for all the reasons mentioned, including differences in class power, which determines wage levels of a group. Once all barriers to education and training are eliminated, e.g., the ghetto versus elite private preparatory high schools, labor monopolies removed, e.g., bar exams and deliberate limits on medical school "seats," and class power equated, then we will realize that the skilled labor premium for the CEO or medical doctor are fictitious fetishes. The CEO has higher wages because his class has the power to determine them even though the value of his or her socially necessary labor does not justify the wage. Rather, this wage is a return, a rent, a reward for class power and position. As for the question of why study to be a doctor when you get the same as the janitor, the answer is simple: because schools will be free and you enjoy that versus other jobs—intrinsic rewards, in short. Otherwise how do we explain people training to be priests only to take vows of poverty, let alone PhDs in philosophy? Frankly, I'd rather be seen by a doctor that trained for the love of the profession than by a lover of gold.

Marx was wrong regarding the relationship between complex labor, knowledge, and wages for the same reasons he attributed to Aristotle's inability to deduce the next intellectual step in the labor theory of value. Namely, Aristotle could not see the link between slave labor and value because of his epoch's zeitgeist which was based on slavery. In the same sense, Marx could not see the difference between knowledge, wage, and labor because he too was limited by his corresponding zeitgeist of hierarchical relations (in this case social, not just economic) which led him to see labor as "stratified" from the simple to the complex, with corresponding wage levels, e.g., the artisan versus unskilled worker. After all, how could his, a doctor's, or attorney's labor be equated to that of the janitor's? But, if we are all equal, then we are all equally necessary or unnecessary. For example, can the medical doctor build her house, educate her children, sweep the streets, dispose of garbage, and produce her own clothing? Can a lawyer or college professor build her own automobile, laptop, or furniture? Why do US medical doctors earn more than their Polish counterparts for the same exact labor?

Although there is such a thing as use value,[91] real value is something different, as is "cost." Value is not what someone is willing to pay for something. Rather value has its foundation in knowledge. Everything derives value from the knowledge reflected in its creation, while labor is the tool for giving form to knowledge in the physical world. Cost is understood as the expenditure of resources to produce or reproduce something. Labor's only cost is what it takes for it to survive and reproduce itself; beyond that labor has no value. The reason we or Marx thought labor had value was because of its artificial commodification. Similarly, Marx was wrong in thinking that machines represent stored labor. Instead, they represent accumulated knowledge. Since labor has no value, neither do machines—beyond the material cost of creating them. Value is to be found only in the knowledge that made it possible for humans to create mechanical copies of their productive abilities. Now machines can provide most of the labor required to run society. Since it is the pool of accumulated societal knowledge (which is part of the commons or society's total wealth) that made the creation of these machines possible, then they are also part of the commons to which we all have right to. And, if these machines are owned by everyone, we will be free to pursue other creative activities.

Beyond the cost to reproduce it, labor cost per unit can be set at whatever level of compensation is socially agreed upon, regardless of whose labor it is. The maximum hourly labor compensation, in turn, is determined by what a society can bear, which is predetermined by the material development and available resources. In short, the overall productive capacity determines the wage level or price for a unit of labor, which means it also determines the average standard of living. Consequently, so long as one contributes to the socially necessary time to keep society running, e.g., three hours per day, then one would be compensated equally to everyone else. Keep in mind that in such a system a three-hour workday with a three- to four-day workweek would be considered full-time, earning a standard annual income much like forty hours of work today for full-time income. In essence this is how you divide resources equitably once the means of production have been returned to the commons. Of course, there could always be allowances and adjustments in the system to reflect divergent needs based on disabilities, old age, etc. These are details to be worked out by the citizens themselves. More importantly, since we would be given units or credits in compensation for our labor, which we would be free to use for obtaining goods and services we desire, then this system would also maintain a guiding function of prices. This means individual choice still determines what a society will produce and how much, in contrast to central planning. But, unlike the capitalist guiding function of prices that are based on unequal wages, in this system peoples' needs would be met first, before luxuries are produced, given the equality of compensation.

Second, historically societies have gone from commodity barter to commodity money to fiat money to paychecks. Today, with direct deposit, many people are not even receiving physical paychecks in their hands, let alone actual cash. And how do we make payments? It is all put on credit and debit cards paid online from our checking accounts where our direct deposit paychecks are deposited. When did you get to physically touch that paycheck? Never! It is all digitized numbers moving around in the debt-credit, electronic, virtual banking balance sheet. This also means that payments for production (wages) and consumption (prices) are made electronically without actual money exchanging hands. Thus, postmodern capitalism has its own *electronic* seeds of destruction: the online banking system.

The online banking system is what could eventually become the basis of a libertarian socialist system of payment and credit or simply distribution. The importance and problem now becomes changing the conceptual basis that those paychecks and prices represent. We could say ten credits pay is what you get for one hour's community work while a loaf of bread costs one credit. Yes, this sounds like restating the market system but we are now de-linking the cognitive association of what money means. Now it is "I help out the community for an hour at ten credits to get what I need" versus "I work for private interests for a wage with which I can buy what I want from another private source." Once we de-link the number, i.e. ten, from the concept of dollars for wages and link it to the concept of credits for community contribution, and de-link price from purchases and link credit to sharing and meeting needs, then it becomes possible to start de-linking those radical concepts even further. For example, the *amount* of credit will become irrelevant to the concept of credit for both the production and consumption transactions. When the amount is not needed and there is no concept of credit, we will be witnessing the psychological withering of a capitalist mode of thinking toward functional alternative forms of societal organization, be it libertarian socialist or whatever else. In short we need an evolution in the patterns of thought to come to the simple conclusion that "I contribute to society my honest fair share because society *is* me which takes care of me," and we would be defining society as the global family of humanity and the "me" as the re-fusing of civil society and public good. In other words, this requires trust in the system. In fact, it was always trust that allowed societies to move through every evolutionary step from barter to direct deposit. This is why we need the habituation of the citizen to these new forms of societal organization, which takes time and education together for all.

In the meantime, a price system defined in different terms would still exist, providing a guiding and rationing function and equitable distribution that people can understand (see t_2, Figure 4). Admittedly, procedurally this may not seem revolutionary because it's not supposed to be. Rather, it provides people with a working economic model. What is revolutionary is the changing concept of prices and wages. By altering these concepts the model provides time for people to become familiarized with a new system without altering their entire lives overnight. Such sudden change often results in anomie while an evolutionary approach habituates people with alternative modes of thought and provides real-world experience with an alternative functioning economy. Finally, this approach would help people move away from capitalist consumption based on *wants* which are insatiable and thus would lead to a straining of societal resources to meet them if these were not limited by the ability to pay. Instead, we would move toward consumption based on need and use which is limited, thus not straining our finite resources.

The Ability to Evolve

Many systems can evolve; the question is at what cost and for whom; Few would disagree with capitalism's ability to evolve. However, its' ability to adapt to change is distorted since it is based on the price mechanism combined with unequal wage incomes that are often artificially determined, as through regionally or globally segmented labor markets.[92] In addition, although capitalism does evolve, we need to consider at what cost to society at large. For example, Polanyi demonstrated the devastating effects of sudden radical change.[93] Although he was writing about the disastrous effects of moving toward capitalism, the work still provides insight as to the social cost of capitalism's evolution.

Today we are continuing to witness capitalism's transformation into a neoliberal global system. However, the social costs are still high for most of the planet's population. Globally, segmented labor markets and contingent labor carry equally high costs for individuals in terms of stress and alienation, and for society in terms of inadequate aggregate demand caused by insufficient purchasing power. Thus, although capitalism is capable of evolution and survival, it does so at the expense of the great majority of society. Therefore, the superior system would be one that can be flexible without the socially devastating consequences needed to support it.

A socialist libertarian society would have a more flexible economic system. Politically, self-governance assures decision making that reflects people's direct needs and beliefs without being filtered through unresponsive professional politicians and ossified political institutions controlled by elite interests. The elimination of special interests by self-governance also assures that the economic system adapts according to social needs. Instead, today we have a skewing of the economy to benefit corporations.[94] In addition, there is greater acceptance of economic change when people know that their living standards would not be adversely affected. For example, in a socialist libertarian society, workers of a floppy disk factory would be more accepting of their plant closing due to obsolescence if they knew their livelihoods would be socially guaranteed and alternative socially necessary work provided. Finally, capitalism's driving motivation is oppression and the desire to escape it through market success—the dominant ideology. Unfortunately, this is a statistical improbability for the majority of the population. Socialist libertarianism's driving force is creative pursuit, since freedom from want and wage slavery would be guaranteed for all.

However, there are specific preconditions in order for the working class to reject the exploitative relations of production and consumption under capitalism in favor of societal change toward greater levels of egalitarianism. First, the legitimacy of the dominant ideology would have to be challenged with a radical *counter ideology* to erode the underpinnings of existing production-consumption relations.[95] Second, class consciousness and solidarity would have to be raised with transformative *societal education* disseminated through independent workers' media, educational institutions, e.g., universities, and art. Societal education would also serve to increase the intensity of class conflict and therefore the impetus for meaningful radical change. Third, targeted *direct action* would be required to alter the relations in production and consumption and thus the mode of production itself. Finally, change would have to be evolutionary so as to avoid societal dislocations or the emergence of a new exploitative class. Ideally, this would provide time to develop and acquire functioning alternatives to existing socioeconomic relations and authoritarian social structures that would benefit humanity rather than an elite few.

Next, chapter three examines past forms of resistance drawing from the old radical labor and civil rights movements respectively. The chapter also demonstrates how these movements were built based on radical counter ideology, societal education, independent media, and militant direct action, including full-blown rebellion. It is argued that these are exactly the same tools and strategies that the working class needs to adopt and adapt today to build a new far-reaching socioeconomic rights movement.

Notes

1. Chomsky and Pateman, 2005: 149.
2. Domhoff, 2010.
3. Chomsky, 1994, 2002; Greenwald, 2004.
4. Chomsky, 1989; Domhoff, 2010, 1975; Mills, 2000 [1956]; Palast, 2004.
5. McMichael, 2008; O'Hara, 2004.

6. The dominant ideology, in Marxist theory, is the set of common values and beliefs shared by most people in a given society, framing how the majority think about a range of topics. The dominant ideology reflects, or serves, the interests of the dominant class in that society. If the dominant ideology conflicted with the legitimacy of the dominant class's rule, then society would have to be in a state of war with itself, with the dominant class appearing as an illegitimate occupation. One way to understand Marxist revolutionary praxis is that it seeks to achieve just that situation of social unrest in which the ruling class is seen as illegitimate—a necessary precursor to achieving the aim of overthrowing the dominant class of capitalism, the bourgeoisie. The ideology of the working class has to achieve dominance, in order for the working class to become the dominant class.

7. See Domhoff, 1975, and Mills, 2000 [1956]). According to Marx, people may not be self-conscious of their "class" and its common interests. In this case it is only a class "in themselves"—they simply exist. When people become aware of their common class interests and organize to actively promote them then they become a class "for themselves." Here the elite have been and are extremely class conscious and act on their own interests.

8. "Interlocking directorate" refers to members of a corporate board of directors serving on the boards of multiple corporations. A direct interlock occurs when two firms share a director or when an executive of one firm sits on the board of a second firm. An indirect interlock occurs when two corporations have directors who each also serve on the board of a third firm. Interlocks allow for upper-class cohesion, coordinated action, and unified political-economic power. They allow corporations to increase their influence by exerting power as a group, and to work together toward common goals. Also, they help the upper class maintain a class advantage, and gain more power over workers and consumers, by reducing intra-class competition and increasing cooperation. Interlocks act as communication channels, enabling information to be shared between boards via multiple directors who have access to inside information for multiple companies. They also benefit the involved companies due to reduced competition and increased information. Some theorists believe that because multiple directors often have interests in firms in different industries, they are more likely to think in terms of general corporate class interests, rather than simply the narrow interests of individual corporations.

9. Mariolis, 1975; Mintz and Schwartz, 1985; US Senate Committee on Governmental Affairs, 1978b.
10. Domhoff, 2010.
11. US Senate Committee on Governmental Affairs, 1978a.
12. Domhoff, 2010; Mizruchi, 1992.
13. Giroux, 2007.
14. Domhoff, 2010.
15. Palast, 2004.
16. The uniform net capital rule was created by the US Securities and Exchange Commission (SEC) in 1975 to regulate directly the ability of broker-dealers to meet their financial obligations to customers and other creditors. Broker-dealers are companies that trade securities for customers (i.e., brokers) and for their own accounts (i.e., dealers). The rule requires those firms to value their securities at market prices and to apply to those values a haircut (i.e., a discount) based on each security's risk characteristics. The haircut values of securities are used to compute the liquidation value of a broker-dealer's assets to determine whether the broker-dealer holds enough liquid assets to pay all its non-subordinated liabilities and to still retain a cushion of required liquid assets (i.e., the "net capital" requirement) to ensure payment of all obligations owed to customers if there is a delay in liquidating the assets. On April 28, 2004, the SEC voted unanimously to permit the largest broker-dealers (i.e., those with "tentative net capital" of more than $5 billion) to apply for exemptions from this established haircut method. Upon receiving SEC approval, those firms were permitted to use mathematical models to compute the haircuts on their securities based on international standards used by commercial banks. Since 2008, many commentators on the financial crisis of 2007 have identified the 2004 rule change as an important cause on the basis that it permitted certain large investment banks (i.e. Bear Stearns, Goldman Sachs, Lehman Brothers, Merrill Lynch, and Morgan Stanley) to increase dramatically their leverage (i.e., the ratio of their debt or assets to their equity).
17. Domhoff, 2009.
18. Chomsky, 1989, 1994, 2002; Goodman and Dretzin, 2005.
19. Chomsky, 1989, 2002; Greenwald, 2004.
20. McMichael, 2008.
21. Chomsky, 1989, 1994, 2002; Goodman and Dretzin, 2005.
22. Chomsky and Pateman, 2005: 160.
23. Greenwald, 2004.
24. McLaren and Leonard, 1992; McLaren, 2005; McLaren, et al., 2009.

25. Giroux, 2007.
26. Chomsky and Pateman, 2005: 171.
27. Kozol, 1992, 2005.
28. Attwell and Lavin, 2007; King and Bannon, 2002.
29. McLaren et al., 2009.
30. Gramsci distinguished between a "traditional" intelligentsia which sees itself (wrongly) as a class apart from society, and the thinking groups which every class produces from its own ranks "organically." Such "organic" intellectuals do not simply describe social life in accordance with scientific rules, but rather articulate, through the language of culture, the feelings and experiences which the masses could not express for themselves. The need to create a working-class culture relates to Gramsci's call for a kind of education that could develop working-class intellectuals, who would not simply introduce Marxist ideology from without the proletariat, but rather renovate and make critical of the status quo the already existing intellectual activity of the masses. His ideas about an education system for this purpose correspond with the notion of critical pedagogy and popular education as theorized and practiced in later decades by Paulo Freire in Brazil (see McLaren and Leonard, 1992).
31. McLaren, 2005.
32. Gramsci, 1971; Weber, 1978 [1922].
33. Weber, 1978 [1922].
34. Rocker, 1938.
35. Gramsci, 1971.
36. Guerin, 1970; Rocker, 1938.
37. Guerin, 1970; Rocker, 1938; Ward, 1982.
38. Kropotkin, 2005 [1892].
39. Wikipedia, http://en.wikipedia.org/wiki/Libertarian_socialism.
40. Domhoff, 2010.
41. Guerin, 1970.
42. Rocker, 1938: 112–113.
43. Mishel et al., 2003–2009; Peck, 2002; Wolfson, 2003; Young, 2006.
44. Rocker, 1938: 111–112.
45. Kotz, McDonough, and Reich 1994.
46. Kotz, McDonough, and Reich 1994; Marx, 1978a [1867], 1978b [1862–63].
47. Wolfson 2003.
48. Ibid., 261.
49. Clawson, 2003; Silver, 2003.
50. Marx, 1978c: 4–5.

51. Aronowitz, 2005; Mishel et al., 2003–2009.
52. Gramsci famously stated that all people are intellectuals, in that all have intellectual and rational faculties, but not all people have the social function of intellectuals.
53. Class consciousness is to be conscious of one's social class or economic rank in society. In Marxist theory, it refers to the self-awareness, or lack thereof, in which case it becomes "false class consciousness," of a particular class; its capacity to act in its own rational interests; or its awareness of the historical tasks implicit to it.
54. Marx, 1973 [1858].
55. Rocker, 1938.
56. Weber, 1978 [1922].
57. Althusser, 2001.
58. In other words, critical education is in itself a revolutionary act. See, for example, Giroux 1988; Macrine et al., 2009.
59. Ward, 1982: 14.
60. Brecher, 1997.
61. Gramsci, 1971.
62. Rocker, 1938.
63. As cited in Guerin, 1970.
64. Dahrendorf, 1959.
65. Ibid., 212.
66. Polanyi, 2001 [1944].
67. As cited in Chomsky and Pateman, 2005: 151.
68. Gramsci, 1971.
69. Guerin, 1970: 152–53.
70. Gramsci, 1971.
71. Gramsci, 1971; Giroux, 1988; McLaren and Jaramilo, 2009.
72. Dahrendorf, 1959.
73. Giroux, 2007.
74. Chomsky, 1989, 1994, 2002; Domhoff, 2010; Greenwald, 2004.
75. Giroux, 1988.
76. Giroux, 2007.
77. Proudhon, 1980 [1863].
78. Rocker, 1938: 73.
79. Rogers and Streeck, 1994.
80. Ibid., 100.
81. Ibid., 101.
82. In economics, an externality is a cost or benefit, not transmitted through prices, incurred by a third party who did not participate in the

transaction causing the cost or benefit. A benefit is called a positive externality and a cost is a negative externality. In these cases, in a competitive market, prices do not reflect the full costs or benefits of producing or consuming a product or service. Producers and consumers may either not bear all of the costs or not reap all of the benefits of the economic activity, causing too much or too little of the good to be produced or consumed in terms of overall costs and benefits to society. For example, manufacturing that causes air pollution imposes costs on the whole society, while fire-proofing a home improves the fire safety of neighbors. If there exist external costs such as pollution, the good will be overproduced by a competitive market, as the producer does not take into account the external costs when producing the good. If there are external benefits, such as with education, too little of the good would be produced by private markets as producers and buyers do not take into account the external benefits to others. Here overall cost and benefit to society is defined as the sum of the economic benefits and costs for all parties involved.

83. In economics, "free riders" are those who consume more than their fair share of a public resource, or shoulder less than a fair share of the costs of its production. Free riding is usually considered to be an economic problem when it leads to the non-production or underproduction of a public good (and thus to Pareto inefficiency), or when it leads to the excessive use of a common property resource. The free rider problem is the question of how to limit free riding (or its negative effects) in these situations.

84. Gramsci, 1971; Guerin, 1970; Proudhon, 1980 [1863]; Ward, 1982.
85. Brecher, 1997; Chomsky and Pateman, 2005.
86. Mishel et al., 2003–2009.
87. As cited in Guerin, 1970.
88. Ibid.
89. Because our wants are insatiable and resources are limited, every society must ration the distribution of goods and services based on certain principles such as capitalist, socialist, or communal ones.
90. Bebchuk and Fried, 2006; Burton and Weller, 2005.
91. Use value is the utility derived from consuming a good or service.
92. The concept of globally segmented labor markets was developed by Asimakopoulos who argues that corporations using their control over governments and the principles of global trade and financial regimes have segregated the world's workers into two regions. One region is the democratic West (or global North), based on consumption with high wages and living standards, the other is made up of poor, often

nondemocratic nations like China, based on authoritarian production with low wages and living standards.
93. Polanyi, 2001 [1944].
94. Zepezauer, 2004.
95. Gramsci, 1971.

3

Societal Education: The Violent Labor Movement & The Civil Rights *Rebellion*

"The Committee has, after mature deliberation, decided to organize their forces on a truly military basis."
Homestead Strikers Committee

"The Ballot or the Bullet"
Malcolm X

The labor movement in the United States is little more than a disorganized, motley crew of unions and activist groups. The old radical labor movement has been absorbed into the institutional framework of the capitalist system. Now, instead of leading the militant rank and file, labor leaders suppress them;[1] in order to obtain contracts, unions gave up the right to strike; more important, labor gave up on political action that would challenge the ideological hegemony of capitalism.[2] It opted instead for Samuel Gompers' model of business unionism[3] while aligning itself with the Democratic Party. However, any genuine labor movement must resist private productive property.[4] By accepting the institutionalization of class conflict, workers have de facto submitted to capitalist principles, thus legitimizing an inherent ideology of control and inequality.[5]

Using the struggle for the eight-hour workday and civil rights as case studies, the radical pre-1940s labor and 1960s–'70s civil rights movements are reviewed through a libertarian socialist framework in search of class actions that can increase working-class gains. Evidently, the old labor and civil rights movements obtained many of their gains by challenging the dominant ideology with their own radical *counter ideology* emanating from socialists, anarchists, and other radical activists; they created mass support through *societal education,* engaging in *direct action,* civil disobedience, violent resistance, and even full-scale revolts. Overall, meaningful gains were not obtained peacefully through a political process or provided voluntarily by the elite. Concessions were achieved through violent resistance and revolt.

The historical record suggests that the working class would obtain greater gains today through direct action and ideological challenges to capitalism instead of working exclusively within the capitalist institutional and legal framework. However, this requires building a new movement that will incorporate a strategy of societal education, economic civil disobedience, and resistance to state violence. Economic civil disobedience is defined as disobeying anti-labor and anti-consumer laws with militant and even revolutionary direct action and the determination to violently resist state violence. This strategy combines Thoreau's[6] classic analysis of civil disobedience with direct action, defined as the use of sabotage, strikes, workplace occupations, boycotts, beatings of elites, mass movements, and revolutions.[7]

Leaving aside the impact of immigration, globalization, class cleavages, new technologies, and historical circumstances such as 9/11, the working class has always faced severe obstacles, and while these may change, the fundamental principles governing distribution have not. For example, is the Patriot Act more restrictive of radical working-class direct action today compared to the nineteenth-century legislation that outlawed even forming a union or the routine use of armed forces to subdue working-class actions, with dozens of casualties? It is acknowledged that the current environment allows militant working-class direct action to be branded as terrorist by the state and elite who are the true terrorists.[8] However, societal education can inform the public that the state is part of the problem and that a legitimate societal movement may, if pressed, have to resort to violence when alternative means of peaceful resolution have been exhausted. One need look no further than Thomas Jefferson, who encouraged revolution against oppressive governments. He clearly stated that this should not be confused with treason as governments can become corrupt and the very act of revolution would indeed be patriotic.

This, to some extent, was also what spurred the civil rights revolutions as a supplement to legislative efforts when the latter were blocked by a clearly racist state including Democrats and Republicans alike. In fact, the state itself has routinely used violence as a legitimate means to an end as with the War of Independence, World War I, and World War II, when violence was seen as the only alternative to capitulation, not to mention wars of empire such as Vietnam or Iraq. When the working class engaged in radical action, it was the state which was mostly responsible for using violence. This was why protesters would find it necessary to arm themselves for self-defense against state-directed military suppression. Unfortunately, history indicates that such extreme levels of conflict are still necessary today.[9]

THE VIOLENT LABOR MOVEMENT

First, history has proven that societal education increases class consciousness and solidarity within the working class, which in turn increase the intensity of class conflict and therefore the chances for radical change. Second, when attempting to obtain and maintain meaningful gains, the working class has had to engage in self-defense against violent suppression by the state. Moreover, when the labor movement engaged in direct action, its failures were due to the overwhelming use of military force. In cases where labor's actual or perceived force and determination exceeded that of the state, concessions were made. There is also increasing theoretical and empirical evidence that violent direct action results in greater concessions for the disprivileged from the state and employers than does political action alone.[10] The review of the struggle for the eight-hour workday supports these arguments. However, when labor did not engage in radical action the outcome was the formation of policies and legal structures that disprivilege the working class and institutionalize its defeat. This has been demonstrated during the past forty years by the lack of radical action, resulting in significant reductions of working-class attainments.[11]

What could be done to spur radical actions? According to anarchists such as Bakunin, Malatesta, and Proudhon, the basis for action is societal education.[12] For example, Gramsci argued in his theory of hegemony that a precondition for socialism includes the ideological development of a feasible alternative or counter-hegemony to existing forms of societal organization.[13] This would be accomplished through the objective societal education of the working class and experience functioning with alternative forms of organization. Rocker also emphasized worker education as a precondition for action.[14] Thus, this book address the motivational basis for the working class to engage in economic civil disobedience through societal education to increase class consciousness and in turn, solidarity—minimizing working-class cleavages—that can then be transformed into direct action. This is summarized as education, class consciousness, solidarity, action.

Societal Education and Class Consciousness

What made direct action by the old labor movement possible were programs of societal education including an independent media, schools, art, and socio-political organizations.[15] Although many working-class organizations and unions often experienced internal disagreement over how to allocate limited resources between societal education and other activities, nevertheless funds would be made available for the former. It was through this outreach to the general public that labor was able to get its message out, raise class consciousness, and obtain broad community support for direct action along Gramscian principles of developing a counter-hegemony.[16] It is characteristic that historically the mainstream media would misrepresent and attack labor while exhorting violent actions by police, the National Guard, and federal troops.[17] Consequently, it was fortuitous that the labor movement had its own independently owned and operated media outlets. By the early 1900s there were over 323 socialist publications, ranging from daily to monthly newspapers to academic publications with a circulation of over two million.[18] There were also at least three national publications: *Appeal to Reason*, the *National Rip-Saw*, and the *International Socialist Review*, with a combined circulation of roughly one million.[19]

Also at this time, labor unions, socialist parties, and other worker organizations would establish and support schools, college programs, and a host of worker education programs.[20] Among these were the Worker Education Bureau, which was affiliated with forty labor schools; the Highlander Folk School; the Rand School of Social Science; the Brookwood Labor College; the Commonwealth Labor College; and Work Peoples' College. The last two even offered full-time residential programs. These schools would train future labor leaders, teach workers how to organize, and raise class consciousness.

Beyond training in the above milieus, songs, theater, film, and literature were also employed by the labor movement to promote class consciousness and solidarity.[21] In terms of literature and theater there were Upton Sinclair with novels like *The Jungle*, Clifford Odets' *Waiting for Lefty*, and a host of plays performed around the country by labor colleges and groups such as Brookwood, which had three companies. Also, "For ten cents, workers could find themselves heroically portrayed in stories like *Larry Locke: Man of Iron, or, A Fight for Fortune, A Story of Labor and Capital*, and *Jasper Ray: The Journeyman Carpenter, or, One Man as Good as Another in America*."[22] Furthermore, songs such as "Solidarity Forever" and "Father Was Killed by the Pinkerton Men" have been recognized by the labor movement as some of the most moving and powerful. It has been said that the IWW—an anarchist labor union—were the "singingest" American union.[23] It is worth noting that the organizations which had the most voluminous and passionate song repertoires were those which faced higher levels of conflict, such as industrial unions like the IWW. In contrast, more peaceful craft unions of the time like the American Federation of Labor (AFL) lacked virtually any songs. Thus, through the arts, labor raised class consciousness while the participatory nature and themes of the work promoted solidarity.[24]

There was even a vibrant Socialist Party headed by the charismatic Eugene Debs, who argued, as Gramsci, that people had to understand socialism before they supported it.[25] More important, "two major anarcho-communist groups had followings greater than that of the SLP [Socialist Labor Party] in the mid-eighties—the Social Revolutionaries, led by Johann Most, and the Home Club of the Knights of Labor, whose fifty members were all leading officers of local assemblies in New York City."[26] Overall, a host of anarchist and other radical groups produced leaders which in turn would infiltrate unions and political parties, providing ideological leadership while encouraging agitation. Often these radical leaders faced government persecutions and executions as with August Spies, Albert Parsons, Adolph Fischer, and George Engel, who were hanged on November 11, 1887, after being falsely convicted for the Haymarket Square bombing. In addition, radical leaders, who were widely respected by the rank and file, were purged even by union officials who saw them as a threat to their own power.

Violent Times and Solidarity

In order to understand how the working class obtained specific demands, it is important to understand the broader social context of the times, which were characterized by high levels of intense and violent class conflict. Societal education, and the high levels of class consciousness and solidarity which it produced, made it possible for the old labor movement to engage in violent direct actions in defiance of law, challenging private productive property and state authority, even turning into full-blown revolts with worker self-organization and self-directed economic activity. The typical state response was to deploy troops, shoot protesters, and violate the law itself. These full-fledged battles were supplemented by extrajudicial executions of labor leaders and left-wing witch hunts and purges. Attacks on strikers were answered by workers and citizens with battles of resistance using clubs, knives, rifles, dynamite, and even cannons.[27] This is exemplified by the historical record of the Great Railroad Strike of 1877;[28] the Pennsylvania Homestead Strike of 1892;[29] the Illinois Pullman Strike of 1894;[30] the Seattle general strike of 1919;[31] and the Flint Sit-Down Strike of 1936–37.[32] These strikes led to a de facto functioning state of libertarian socialism where worker-citizens directed their own production and operated their own cities.

The old labor movement was able to engage in mass strikes despite significant obstacles such as injunctions and armed suppression by the state. For example, the Great Railroad Strike of 1877 spread from Texas to New York, and involved tens of thousands of workers in multiple cities.[33] The Pullman Strike of 1894 involved twenty-seven states and over 260,000 workers.[34] Although these strikes originated within specific companies or industries, they quickly spread to other industries in the form of *sympathy or secondary strikes*. Inter- and intra-industry sympathy strikes were common as an effective tool to exact economic costs on the targeted company. They also forced other impacted companies to pressure the targeted firm to resolve the dispute. Thus, strikes were used strategically to raise the overall economic cost of labor disputes not only for particular businesses, but for business owners as a *class*. Sympathy strikes also contributed to and demonstrated increasing workers' class consciousness and solidarity.[35]

In addition, the high levels of solidarity and class consciousness in the nineteenth century were exemplified in many cases, although not all, by cutting across racial and ethnic lines.[36] According to Montgomery:

> Because the weakest links in the chain of labor solidarity were found at the points where the white, black, and yellow races met, the numerous episodes of cooperation between white and black workers during the 1880s provided a noteworthy feature of the labor upsurge. . . . The Knights alone had some 60,000 black members by 1886. More than a fifth of the early members of United Mine Workers in the bituminous fields were black. In 1896, Richard L. Davis, a black leader from Ohio, won the highest vote of any candidate for that union's National Executive Board. The New Orleans docks were a stronghold of biracial unionism. When the white scalemen and packers there allied with the black teamsters to strike for a ten-hour day in October, 1892, the city's Board of Trade offered concessions to the whites but refused to negotiate with blacks. In response, forty-nine unions shut down the entire city and kept it shut, despite venomous attacks on the blacks in the local press. In the

end, the Board of Trade capitulated entirely, giving labor one of its greatest victories of the century.[37]

Class consciousness and solidarity were further demonstrated by the high levels of working-class citizen support. In these cases, strikes would often transform into spontaneous armed rebellions along anarchist principles. Communities such as Pittsburgh, St. Louis, and Los Angeles in 1877, Homestead in 1892, Pullman in 1894, Seattle in 1919, and Flint in 1936 were taken over by citizens who engaged in self-rule and self-directed production. These actions were often so effective that institutional power holders considered them a challenge to the capitalist system itself. Workers and citizens also armed themselves and organized into military units in order to defend against state reactionary suppressive violence. For example:

> In late July, 1877, train crews on the Baltimore and Ohio Railroad struck against a wage cut, triggering a chain . . . of events which President Hayes was to condemn as an "insurrection." Popular anger over the dispatch of troops to reopen the line spread the strike to Baltimore, where huge crowds clashed with the militia. Simultaneously, work stoppages followed the rail lines across Pennsylvania from both ends of the state into the smallest mill and mining towns. Thousands of Pittsburgh iron workers and other residents defeated soldiers sent from Philadelphia in pitched battle, subsequently burning all property of the Pennsylvania Railroad. Across Ohio and Indiana, workers' committees simply took over their towns, halting all work until their demands were met by employers. A quickly organized strike in Chicago brought troops and artillery to the city, and shots rang out at the Halstead Street viaduct. In St. Louis, thousands of workers closed down the city's industry for several days. Governmental authorities fled the town.[38]

In 1892, Homestead's governance was taken over by its armed working class, which organized its own military units:

> The Committee has . . . decided to organize their forces on a truly military basis. The force of four thousand men has been divided into three divisions or watches, each of these divisions is to devote eight hours of the twenty-four to the task of watching the plant. The Commanders of these divisions are to have as assistants eight captains composed of one trusted man from each of the eight local

lodges. These Captains will report to the Division Commanders, who in turn will receive the orders of the Advisory Committee. . . . The girdle of pickets will file reports to the main headquarters every half hour, and so complete and detailed is the plan of campaign that in ten minutes' time the Committee can communicate with the men at any given point within a radius of five miles. In addition to all this, there will be held in reserve a force of 800 Slavs and Hungarians. The brigade of foreigners will be under the command of two Hungarians and two interpreters.[39]

The *Chicago Tribune* called the Pullman situation in 1894 an "insurrection."[40] Meanwhile, in the same year in Los Angeles, Attorney General Olney was warned of pending open rebellion while the commander of the US troops in Chicago, General Nelson Miles, believed the US government itself was in danger of being overthrown.[41] Ultimately, the striking workers at Pullman were defeated because of overwhelming state military forces:

By early July, a total strike had settled in over the railroads of the middle and far West, bringing in quick sequence a federal injunction against the strike, the stationing of troops at all vital junctions of the lines, martial law in Chicago, and the imprisonment of Debs and other strike leaders. . . . After intense debate, the leaders advised their members not to strike, noting the "array of armed force and brutal monied aristocracy," represented by "United States Marshals, injunctions of courts, proclamations by the President, and . . . bayonets of soldiers."[42]

Following the "insurrection" described above, the city of Seattle in 1919 was taken over by its citizens, leading Mayor Ole Hanson to call it "an attempted revolution which they [the strikers] attempted to spread all over the United States."[43] Subsequent to Seattle, in Flint in 1936, the city manager was literal when he stated "we are going down there shooting. The strikers have taken over this town and we are going to take it back."[44]

Workers would also blow up factories and buildings to exact an economic toll upon capitalists. Pittsburgh in 1877 saw over 2,000 railroad cars burn while citizens made sure the fire did not spread to nearby tenements.[45] The attack on private business property also included mass lootings. Strikers assisted by townspeople would capture railroad cars, distributing their contents to the masses. In other instances, citizens would appropriate and operate businesses under their own management, as in the Seattle general strike of 1919.[46] According to the *Seattle Union Record*:

> The closing down of the capitalistically controlled industries of Seattle, while the WORKERS ORGANIZE to feed the people, to care for the babies and the sick, to preserve order—THIS will move them, for this looks too much like the taking over of POWER by the workers. Labor will not only SHUT DOWN the industries, but Labor will REOPEN, under the management of the appropriate trades, such activities as are needed to preserve public health and public peace. If the strike continues, Labor may feel led to avoid public suffering by reopening more and more activities, UNDER ITS OWN MANAGEMENT.[47]

Therefore, engaging in mass revolt had the impact of challenging the upper class not only financially but also politically. When entire cities were run and operated directly by their citizens, it became a real-life experiment in anarchist self-organization as with the Spanish Revolution of 1936. More importantly, it became a functioning example of alternative politico-economic forms of societal organization. This is why the elite would often have to regain control of entire regions through military expeditions against the American people in the name of capitalist private property rights.

The Eight-hour Workday

The US history of the eight-hour workday demonstrates that working-class gains were obtained through violent direct action with legislation forced to follow accomplished facts on the ground. An early promoter of the eight-hour movement was Ira Steward, who lived in 1860s Boston. With the Civil War as the background, Steward's ideology was abolitionist, recognizing that labor's interests cut across race and ethnicity. A number of prominent eight-hour activists like George E. McNeill, Edward H. Rogers, and Wendell Phillips also recognized the importance of class solidarity inclusive of race.[48] The movement was fueled by numerous eight-hour leagues and unions which relied primarily on working through the legislative process with signed petitions, lobbying, and supporting candidates for the eight-hour workday. Strikes supplemented the agitation as a secondary tool. Originally, the movement focused on state legislatures rather than the federal government.

In 1864, Chicago became the center of the fight for an eight-hour workday. By 1865 there were six eight-hour demonstrations which included 67,000 workers in Northeastern states, while 4,000 people marched in Chicago.[49] In response, Illinois was the first state to pass eight-hour legislation in 1867, which in practice proved virtually ineffective. Workers in Chicago reacted with a demonstration numbering 10,000 declaring a general strike on May 1, 1867, which brought the city's economy to a standstill. Troops were called in and the strike was broken. In 1868, congress responded with a law which provided an eight-hour day to some federal employees. Unfortunately, all these legislative measures lacked enforcement mechanisms, prompting the National Labor Union to declare in 1867 that eight-hour laws "have been passed by the legislatures [but] . . . for all practical purposes they might as well have never been placed on the statute books, and can only be described as frauds on the labouring class."[50]

In response to the political defeats of 1867–68, Steward and the labor leaders realized the importance of societal education in order to obtain broader support. This signaled a shift away from the failed legislative process into one favoring a more radical approach based on direct action cultivated by societal education through eight-hour leagues, social clubs, and union halls.

For example, New York passed eight-hour laws in 1867 in response to threats of massive strikes by New York City workers. By 1872, the ineffectiveness of the laws also prompted massive strikes in Philadelphia, Buffalo, Chicago, Jersey City, and Albany. In New York City 100,000 workers went on strike demanding eight-hour laws be enforced. The agitation was led by the anarchist International Workers' Association (IWA), Marxists, and various radical leaders, winning an effective eight-hour workday for the building trades, resulting in victory marches involving 150,000 people. These victories, together with the historical ineffectiveness of eight-hour state laws, led the Federation of Organized Trades and Labor Unions (FOTLU), predecessor of the AFL, to demand with direct action an eight-hour workday. This was after President Chester Arthur in an 1881 meeting with FOTLU delegates refused to enforce the federal eight-hour law. This prompted the FOTLU to issue a resolution in 1885:

> It would be in vain to expect the introduction of the eight-hour rule through legislative measures . . . [A] united demand to reduce the hours of labor, supported by a firmly established and determined organization, would be far more effective than a thousand laws, whose

execution depends upon the good will of aspiring politicians or sycophantic department officials . . . the workmen in their endeavor to reform the prevailing economic conditions must rely upon themselves and their own power exclusively.[51]

As a result, workers increased their agitation, escalating the number of strikes and participants dramatically in 1886 (Table 6). Strikers also armed themselves in anticipation of intervention by state and federal troops as was done during the Great Railroad Strike of 1877. "Such brigades of armed workers had grown up in a number of cities, largely in response to the use of police and military forces in 1877. By 1886 they existed . . . in Cincinnati, . . . Detroit, Chicago, St. Louis, Omaha, Newark, New York, San Francisco, Denver, and other cities."[52] It is important to note that leadership for nationally organizing the 1886 agitation was undertaken by a small core of anarchists working together with local craft unions and the relatively small FOTLU. "The [anarcho-] syndicalists provided skilled organizers . . . [they] also made a contribution by organizing armed workers' militias ostensibly capable of defending strikes. . . . they were the lone attempts by a labor organization to speak to what was a prime concern of prospective strikers—the possibility of attacks by private and public police."[53] In contrast, the major national union (the Knights of Labor under Terence Powderly) opposed strikes favoring societal education and the legislative process.

Table 6. Strike Activity 1883–1886

Year	Number of Strikes	Number of Establishments	Participants
1886	1,411	9,891	499,489
1885	645	2,284	242,705
1884	443	2,367	147,054
1883	478	2,759	149,763

Source: Brecher, 1997: 47.

Anticipating the fight for shorter hours, many workers also established eight-hour leagues. The leaders of the leagues included many anarchists, socialists, and revolutionaries. Local unions also began preparations for agitation, despite half-hearted support by national union officials. Prior to May 1886, thousands of workers around the country had already begun agitation by striking and demonstrating. On May 1, there were massive demonstrations in most major cities including Boston, Chicago, Cincinnati, San Francisco, Milwaukee, and New York. As a result of the demonstration of mass force, over 185,000 workers obtained concessions for reduced work hours by their employers in various industries.[54]

It quickly became clear that the working class would be able to exert its power and obtain greater gains than shorter hours. But things came to a halt by May 4 with the Haymarket Square bombing in Chicago. The government used the event as a pretext to crack down on anarchists and other radical leaders behind the agitation. Leaders and strikers were arrested without warrants and held for long periods without charges.[55] Many concluded that the government voided freedom of speech and association. May Day had casualties as well. Protesters and strikers in many cities were confronted by armed state and federal forces. In some cases, troops were given orders to fire on the crowds and they did. For example, Wisconsin's Governor Rusk ordered state troops to shoot protesters in Milwaukee, resulting in the killing of nine; in Chicago, police killed four strikers at the McCormick plant.[56]

Subsequently, the period from 1890 through the early years of the next decade was characterized by legal challenges to eight-hour laws. This limited response was in part due to the chilling effect of the Haymarket crackdown and the elimination of radical anarchist leadership. Another reason was the half-hearted efforts by the AFL under Gompers. Although the AFL declared its intention to fight for the eight-hour workday, as of May 1, 1890, Gompers refused to engage in national agitation. He preferred a strategy of allowing specific local craft unions to act alone, often with no central direction or help.[57]

The biggest reductions in hours were obtained between 1905–1920 through continued direct action.[58] In 1919, for example, 22.5% of the labor force was involved in strikes. The agitation was organized by a small yet radical core of anarchists, including the IWW, that cooperated with local unions while the AFL under Gompers caused more harm than good. For example, the IWW organized successfully the miners' strike of 1906 at Goldfield, Nevada; the successful 1909 "uprising" of 20,000 New York City garment workers; the successful 1912 textile strikes at Lawrence, involving 275,000; the 1913 Paterson silk strikes, involving 25,000, which failed due to police violence and arrests of leadership; the 1916 Mesabi Range strike, involving 10,000. Overall, they were involved in over 150 strikes, including the Coal Wars of 1912–13 in West Virginia and the uprising after the Ludlow Massacre of 1914 where troops using machine guns killed over thirty-two people. The activity of the IWW also prompted Henry Ford's preemptive granting of the eight-hour day and passing of the Adamson Act (1916) extending the eight-hour workday to railroad workers of private companies. The latter was a major success because it was the first time federal law covered workers in private companies. However, the law was passed in response to a pending nationwide strike by 400,000 railroad workers for shorter hours. The government though, used World War I to crack down on anarchist and communist leadership as it did with the Haymarket affair.

By the 1930s, government had to solve the problems of restarting the economy and avoiding revolution due to the Great Depression.[59] According to one journalist in 1933, "capitalism itself was at the point of dissolution."[60] Bank runs and general civil unrest were reaching a crisis point:

> For the first time since the Civil War, armed men patrolled the entrances to federal buildings, while machine gunners perched on rooftops. . . . Unrest was already growing in the farm belt, where mobs had broken up bankruptcy auctions. Four thousand men had occupied the Nebraska statehouse and five thousand stormed Seattle's county building. The governor of North Carolina predicted a violent revolution, and police in Chicago clubbed teachers who had not been paid all school year.[61]

As a result, it was anticipated that Roosevelt's inauguration speech on March 4, 1933 would declare martial law to keep the nation from revolution. This led the New York *Herald-Tribune* on March 5 to print "FOR DICTATORSHIP IF NECESSARY," with other papers running similar headlines.[62]

At the time, the popular consensus held that depression was caused by insufficient purchasing power—ironically, a Marxist argument. Roosevelt felt that an independent union movement would be successful in raising workers' wages, which would then stimulate the economy and ease revolutionary pressures without suspending democracy.[63] However, most union actions, such as establishing or joining a union, engaging in a strike, mass protests, distributing union information, and collective bargaining, were illegal up until this time, taking place in defiance of law. It was not until the Norris-LaGuardia Act (1932) that workers were given basic protections against "yellow dog" contracts—employment on the condition of not joining a union—and injunctions against strikes. Consequently, a number of measures were passed after the Norris-LaGuardia Act as a means of increasing aggregate demand via purchasing power and encouraging union growth. It took the National Labor Relations Act (1935), popularly known as the Wagner Act, to allow workers to legally join unions while forcing employers to recognize collective bargaining. The New Deal also passed legislation establishing the first social safety nets with the Social Security Act (1935).

The government finally legalized the eight-hour workday with the Fair Labor Standards Act (1938) as part of Roosevelt's New Deal. However, it was passed after shorter work hours were de facto won by workers in many industries through often necessarily violent struggles. Overall, these laws had been approved in response to years of agitation with violent direct action. For example, in the midst of the Great Depression, the level of underlying civil unrest was so high that the threat of a popular revolt was believed to be great enough to overwhelm government forces. "With so many banks involved, the U.S. Army—including National Guard and Reserve units—might not be large enough to respond."[64] This was unlike the nineteenth century when government troops usually sufficed to subdue citizen uprisings. As a result of this credible threat of violent revolt against the capitalist system itself, the elites were forced to offer these concessions. "During the Great Depression, the insurgent group (labor) constituted a much larger proportion of the electorate, and therefore left political elites with little choice but to respond to political violence in a beneficent manner."[65] Consequently, the purpose of the New Deal legislation was clearly to alleviate poverty and hardship caused by the depression to avoid a renewed people's revolution such as the ones that took place in the late nineteenth century.[66]

Therefore, the eight-hour workday demonstrates that even basic demands were met only after a prolonged period of agitation from the 1860s to the 1930s, including mass strikes and armed rebellion often led by anarchists.[67] This exemplifies Rocker's argument that even democracies, which represent capitalist interests, did not concede labor rights until after they were confronted by accomplished facts on the ground, resulting from citizens' direct action.[68] It also demonstrates that favorable labor legislation in America has been forced by years of agitation based on direct action and the determination to violently resist state suppression. Strikers were also joined by citizens, often of all races and ethnicities, exemplifying working-class solidarity. Finally, the eight-hour movement demonstrates the important role played by radical leaders and ideology.

THE CIVIL RIGHTS *REBELLION*

Regarding the applicability of the nineteenth century labor strategies to our current situation, some—typically academics—argue that conditions and society have changed, making past strategies and tactics irrelevant.

As long as there is private productive property most people will suffer. That the face of poverty may change does not alter the fact that it still exists because of capitalism. In order to demonstrate the continued effectiveness of militant counter ideology and direct action with the use of violent self-defense we turn to the 1960s and 1970s civil rights movement.

The Civil Rights–Black Power Movement (CRBPM) was successful for the same reasons labor was ultimately successful. It challenged existing dominant ideology with its own radical counter ideology; created mass support by promoting societal education, including through arts, along Gramscian principles; ran and operated its own independent media; and engaged in direct action at the grassroots level with civil disobedience, defensive violence, and revolts. For the working class as a whole this translates into the need to continue the CRBPM with a new citizen rights movement based on a strategy of direct economic civil disobedience and the determination to violently resist reactionary state violence.

Contrary to popular belief, there was nothing *civil* about the civil rights movement. Violent direct action was practiced or threatened by civil rights militants and the Black Power wing of the movement very publicly and in mission statements, e.g., that of the Black Liberation Army. In fact, civil disobedience regularly included nonviolent and violent self-defense proponents espousing radical ideology, e.g., Malcolm X, given the wide spectrum of organizations which would participate in solidarity. And, in addition to earlier classics[69] there is plenty of new evidence that direct action is effective.[70] Furthermore, recent works on the CRBPM also confirm the effectiveness of militant direct action combined with violent self-defense, contrary to perceptions shaped by the corporate media.[71] According to Nell Irvin Painter, a black historian, "without direct action in the 60s much much less would have been accomplished. If getting into the street is the first step, I say get into the street."[72] Indeed, if violence was ineffective then why do governments readily employ it against their own and foreign people?

To understand the importance of direct action and violence in obtaining working-class goals, the CRBPM is reviewed with broad strokes. It will be shown that concessions were not granted willingly. Instead, the use or threat of violent resistance and revolt preceded major concessions. People died, businesses were set ablaze, looting took place, revolts broke out, and civil war even loomed.

Timing of the Period and Intellectual Unity

There is a debate emerging among civil rights and Black Power scholars regarding when these periods began and ended. Traditionally, the *heroic* civil rights era is dated from 1954 to 1965. It is considered distinct from the Black Power era which is seen as emerging later and having negative consequences because of its advocacy of defensive violence. For this work the two eras are considered to be synonymous, dating from the 1950s to the 1970s, despite some clear distinctions:

> Arguing that the "origins" of Black Power rhetoric, ideology, and militancy are to be found by taking a fresh look at ... events during the *heroic period* of the civil rights era, "Black Power studies" transforms civil rights scholarship by placing militant organizers side-by-side with nonviolent moderates. ... Indeed, emerging scholarship suggests that black organizing, protests, conferences, and activism at the local, national and international level *increased* during the first half of the 1970s, a phenomenon that refutes the standard chronology of Black Power, New Left, and other radical social and political movements associated with the 1960s-era political activism.[73]

The groups comprising the CRBPM did not share a singular theoretical ideology. Many were Marxists, Leninists, Maoists, anarchists, Trotskyites, nationalists, and Pan-Africanists just to name a few. In fact, many of these leaders and groups were practicing their own brands or versions of Left ideology as they understood them. However the unifying theme was a militant, (often) leftist and radical ideology. "Black Radicalism contoured these activities [of the CRBPM], providing key intellectual, political, and cultural institutions that nurtured both self-described civil rights and Black Power activists."[74] What is important is that all these schools of thought ultimately represent the same fundamental ideology, namely that the existing structure of society, reflected in the legal code, was underlying many if not all problems, including racism.

This is why practically all civil rights groups were racially integrated—demonstrating class consciousness—including the Black Panther Party, sensitive to the plight of nations such as Vietnam, and critiqued racist capitalism. Furthermore, these groups agreed that in order for meaningful change to occur there would have to be a social movement that would wrest rights from the elite and *their* government. Of course there were also significant differences. For example, some groups believed in integration with broader society while others advocated total secession. Such ideological differences, though, are a powerful feature of Left ideology which is known for its theoretical pluralism. This pluralism to some extent also characterizes capitalism. Although these groups had diverse ideological traditions they were all recognizably "Left" or "progressive." The emphasis on their differences as fundamentally distinct or at odds with other groups ignores their solidarity and is more leftover propaganda aimed at deliberately fractioning these groups via covert programs such as the infamous COINTELPRO. According to Smethurst:

> the coming together of seemingly irreconcilable trends was not as unusual as it seemed; in political centers such as New York City, Marxists and black nationalists fraternized (while maintaining sharp political differences and organizations) and produced activism that "had a certain practical synergy even if they were opposed on an ideological level."[75]

The Civil Rights–Black Power Movement

Looking at the history of the struggle for civil rights we can see that it was not as nonviolent as is commonly thought. Rather, there has been a significant sanitization and repackaging of the civil rights movement by the corporate mass media, as collective memories begin to fade fifty years later. Accordingly, activists were docile and their tactics nonviolent. However, many of the nonviolent marches and protests could only have taken place thanks to the armed protection offered by groups such as the Deacons for Defense and Justice and the Tuscaloosa, Alabama, defense organization. Also, many of the civil rights leaders expressed a militant ideology that in some cases included the belief in violent self-defense and even revolution. The FBI itself considered many civil rights groups and leaders to be a radical threat, targeting them with its covert COINTELPRO[76] program which violated most civil rights protections, not unlike the Patriot Act today.[77] The program's goal was to prevent the rise of an organized nationalist movement of black resistance and to discredit black leaders including Martin Luther King, Stokely Carmichael, and Elijah Muhammad.

First, the civil rights case is a good example of the inadequacy of law which has been mostly conceived, written, promoted, and voted in by capitalist adjuncts. Many civil rights movement actions, such as refusing to sit in the back of a bus, were illegal. Attempts at desegregation by political institutions met with filibusters including by Democrats.[78] Malcolm X, for example, made the following analogy regarding civil rights and law in America which can be applied to labor currently:

> When you go to Washington, D.C. . . . to pass some kind of civil-rights legislation to correct a very criminal situation, what you are doing is encouraging the black man, who is the victim, to take his case into the court that's controlled by the criminal that made him the victim.[79]

Political reform was enacted only after extensive direct violent action threatening to escalate into full-blown revolt. In addition, the government-corporate media propaganda labeled revolts as *riots* to hide their true meaning and historical significance (see Table 7).

Furthermore, the Civil Rights Act of 1964 was signed on July 2 after a long history of lynchings, assassinations, protests, economic boycotts, lootings, revolutionary speeches, and revolts ("riots"). Examples include the Red Summer riots, 1919; Harlem riot, 1935; Montgomery bus boycott, 1955; desegregation at Little Rock, 1957; sit-in campaign, 1960; Freedom Rides, 1961; Mississippi riot, 1962; Birmingham sit-ins, 1963; March on Washington, 1963; Birmingham church bombing, 1963; and Malcolm X giving his speeches "The Ballot or the Bullet" and "The Black Revolution" in 1964. In response to this continued series of actions and violent resistance, the Social Security Act of 1965 (part of Johnson's War on Poverty) and the Voting Rights Act of 1965 (signed on August 6) were passed. However, given that the new laws were practically meaningless in regard to on-the-ground realities, there were yet more protests and deaths: Selma to Montgomery marches and Bloody Sunday, 1965, and the riots of Harlem, Brooklyn, and Philadelphia 1964, Watts in 1965, and Detroit, Newark, and Plainfield in 1967 (see Tables 7 and 8). Overall, the 1960s witnessed over 500 urban rebellions.[80]

Societal Education and Class Consciousness

The civil rights movement also relied heavily on societal education to obtain popular support for direct actions. Organizations such as the Congress of Racial Equality (CORE),[81] the Student Nonviolent Coordinating Committee (SNCC),[82] the United Defense League (UDL),[83]

Table 7. Race Revolts 1917–1977

War and Inter-War Period 1917–1945	
1917	East St. Louis; Chicago
1917	Chester, Pennsylvania
1917	Philadelphia, Pennsylvania
1917	Houston, Texas
Red Summer of 1919	Washington, D.C.
	Chicago, Illinois
	Omaha, Nebraska
	Charleston, South Carolina
	Longview, Texas
	Knoxville, Tennessee
	Elaine, Arkansas
1921	Tulsa, Oklahoma
1923	Rosewood, Florida
1935	Harlem, New York
1943	Detroit, Michigan
1943	Beaumont, Texas
1943	Harlem, New York
1943	Los Angeles, California
Postwar Era 1946–1954	
1946	Columbia, Tennessee, Riot
Civil Rights and Black Power Movement's Period 1955–1977	
1962	Mississippi Riot
1964	Harlem Riot, New York
1964	Philadelphia Race Riot, Pennsylvania
1964	Rochester Race Riot, New York
1965	Watts Riots, Los Angeles, California
1966	Hough Riots, Cleveland, Ohio
1966	Hunter's Point Riot, San Francisco
1966	Chicago Race Riot, Chicago
1966	North Omaha, Nebraska
1967	Texas Southern University Riot, Houston
1967	12th Street Riot, Detroit, Michigan
1967	Buffalo Riot, New York
1967	Milwaukee Riot, Wisconsin
1967	Minneapolis North Side Riots, Minnesota
1967	Newark Riots, New Jersey
1967	Plainfield Riots, New Jersey
1968	Orangeburg Massacre, South, Carolina
Nationwide riots in 125 cities following the assassination of Martin Luther King, Jr.	
1968	Baltimore Riot, Maryland
	West Side Riots, Chicago, Illinois
	Louisville Riots, Kentucky
	Washington, D.C., Riots
	New York City Riots
1969	York, Pennsylvania, Race Riots
1970	Jackson State Killings, Mississippi
1971	Camden Riots, New Jersey
1972–1977	Escambia High Riots in Pensacola, Florida

and the Montgomery Improvement Association (MIA) disseminated information and raised awareness.[84] Most of these groups worked closely with local community organizations, such as churches, and offered training and information through mass meetings. This created powerful grassroots movements via societal education. Finally, some of the organizations, like CORE, used various tactics such as sit-ins, freedom rides, boycotts, etc., which would lead to confrontations and thus generate mainstream news coverage.[85]

Table 8. Key Events of the Civil Rights Movement

1958	Brown v. Board of Education
1955	Murder of Emmett Till
1955–1956	Montgomery Bus Boycott
1957	Desegregating Little Rock
1960	Sit-in Campaign
1961	Freedom Rides
1961–1963	Voter Registration Organizing
1956–1965	Integration of Mississippi Universities
1961–1962	Albany Movement
1963–1964	Birmingham Sit-in Campaign
1963	Birmingham Church Bombing
1963	March on Washington
1964	Mississippi Freedom Summer
1964	Mississippi Freedom Democratic Party
April 1964	Malcolm X Speeches "The Ballot or the Bullet" and "The Black Revolution"
1964	Civil Rights Act of 1964 Signed
1964	Dr. King Awarded Nobel Peace Prize
1965	Boycott of New Orleans by American Football League players
1965	Selma to Montgomery Marches; Bloody Sunday
1965	Voting Rights Act of 1965 signed
1965	The Social Security Act of 1965 signed
1968	Memphis-Assassination of MLK and Poor People's March

These organizations also established over thirty Freedom Schools, local citizenship schools in Mississippi. Volunteers at these schools taught over 3,000 students in 1964. The Highlander Folk School, a labor college where Rosa Parks received training, later became the model for other organizations.[86] As far back as 1959, Bernice Robinson, Septima Clarke, and Esau Jenkins had established citizenship schools in South Carolina with the assistance of Highlander. Overall, these schools not only helped blacks register to vote but also served as a source for teaching leadership skills, critical thinking, and black history. Later the SNCC also organized various voter registration programs with workshops and political lectures.

Art through song, theater, and film was also used as a means of societal learning. Plays such as *The First Militant Preacher* by Ben Caldwell and Amiri Baraka's award-winning *Dutchman* proliferated. The plays were performed by black theater groups like Baraka's Spirit House Movers and Players who sang songs like "Who will Survive America?" More so, the civil rights movement was very active in producing songs to raise awareness such as "We Shall Overcome," "Ain't Gonna Let Nobody Turn Me Around," "Keep Your Eyes on the Prize," and "Oh Freedom." The participatory nature of the songs promoted solidarity and class consciousness, and offered positive images of black empowerment. More importantly, these songs taught people that change was possible.[87] One key figure among many in the civil rights–Black Power artistic movement was Amiri Baraka (LeRoi Jones). Baraka combined art with politics and black identity. In 1965, he founded the short-lived yet influential Black Arts Repertory Theater and School in Harlem, creating the foundation of what became known as the Black Arts Movement (BAM)—the cultural and artistic counterpart of the socioeconomic Black Power Movement. BAM included notable literary figures like Nikki Giovanni, Sonia Sanchez, Maya Angelou, and Rosa Grey. In addition, Baraka formed in Newark, a hotbed of activists, the Spirit House Movers and Players, the United Brothers, and the Committee for a Unified Newark (CFUN). More importantly, Baraka and Sanchez helped establish the first black studies program at San Francisco State University. The importance of the program was that it finally acknowledged a counterperspective within legitimating institutions. In addition, Baraka became pivotal in the promotion of black studies, arguing for an international black identity separated from what he referred to as the murderous US identity.

Overall, many of the artists and performers in BAM were taught and influenced by radical leaders from the civil rights and union movements, most of whom were Left ideologists.[88] This education included left-wing history, theory, politics, and organizing. Thus, militant revolutionary ideology and art grew side by side to form a formidable social movement challenging the existing social structure economically, politically and culturally. Moreover, societal education, as during the old labor movement, increased the *intensity* of class conflict, resulting in the direct actions of the period.

In addition, the civil rights, Black Power, and Black Arts movements were very active in promoting black media such as journals, magazines, and even publishing houses, in addition to theater groups, poetry, music and dance. Through poetry, the movement engaged in education. By owning and operating its own media, the movement could counteract the propaganda of the corporate mainstream media and government. For example, a news broadcast during the 1967 Newark, New Jersey rebellion stated, "It was a long hot riotous summer ... in other major cities civil rights protests blossomed into full-fledged riots that bordered anarchy."[89] This in fact was also the case with the pre-1940s labor movement which owned and operated its own media to counterbalance mainstream anti-labor propaganda. Black media publications included *Freedomways, Liberator*, Rob Williams' newsletter *Crusader*, Paul Robeson's newspaper *Freedom, Muhammad Speaks, Soulbook*, and the *Baltimore African-American*.

Radical Counter Ideology

Many civil rights leaders rejected nonviolence, favoring radical direct action and ideology. Then there was the Black Power Movement exemplified by Malcolm X, Stokely Carmichael, the SNCC,[90] and the Black Panther Party. In addition, there were the militant factions of the civil rights movement that rejected nonviolence in favor of defensive violence such as the Deacons for Defense and Justice,[91] Rob Williams,[92] and CORE. Malcolm X was clearly influential. Despite his controversial and evolving positions there was a basic theme, namely capitalism as the source of black repression. He did not believe the solution to be coalescing into capitalism—as did the Nation of Islam through Black Capitalism[93]—but to radically rearrange power relations by challenging structural inequality by any means, including violent direct action.

He also did not believe that nonviolence was sufficient and had no faith in political institutions.[94] In response to the filibustering of civil-rights legislation he said: "I'm ... one of the 22 million black people who are the victims of democracy, nothing but disguised hypocrisy," a sentiment shared by many working-class people to this day.[95] Instead, he clearly stated that if persuasion through the threat of violence did not work, then actual violence would have to be used against injustice. In fact, he encouraged armed revolt and retaliation for killings of blacks as a means of self-defense:

> There's new strategy coming in. It'll be Molotov cocktails this month, hand grenades next month, and something else next month. It'll be ballots, or it'll be bullets. It'll be liberty, or it will be death. The only difference about this kind of death—it'll be reciprocal. I find you can get a whole lot of small people and whip hell out of a whole lot of big people. They haven't got anything to lose, and they've got every thing to gain. And they'll let you know in a minute: "It takes two to tango; when I go, you go."[96]

Interestingly, this passage echoes the *Communist Manifesto*'s famous declaration "The proletarians have nothing to lose but their chains. They have a world to win. WORKING MEN OF ALL COUNTRIES, UNITE!"[97]

Stokely Carmichael headed the SNCC in 1966. He was known as one of the more articulate proponents of Black Power, and gave a speech by the same title at Berkeley University that year. He and the SNCC had been early practitioners of nonviolent civil disobedience and part of the civil rights movement. By 1965, though, they were disenchanted with Dr. King's nonviolent civil disobedience and adopted a policy of armed self-defense. Eventually, the organization advocated revolution against the institutional power structure. The following excerpts from Carmichael's "Black Power" speech at Berkeley exemplify his Left revolutionary ideology:

> This country is a nation of thieves. It stole everything it has, beginning with black people. The U.S. cannot justify its existence as the policeman of the world any longer. . . . I do not want to be a part of the American pie. The American pie means raping South Africa, beating Vietnam, beating South America, raping the Philippines, raping every country you've been in. I don't want any of your blood money. I don't want to be part of that system. . . . We must question whether or not we want this country to continue being the wealthiest country in the world at the price of raping everybody else. . . . Isn't it hypocritical for Lyndon to talk about how you can't accomplish anything by looting and you must accomplish it by the legal ways? What does he know about legality? . . . "Move on over, or we're going to move over you."[98]

The Deacons for Defense and Justice were formed in Jonesboro Louisiana, in 1964, by ordinary people. The organization did not align with ideological factions. Although they were not part of the Black

Power Movement, they were willing to take up arms in self-defense. The members consisted of black veterans from World War II and Korea. They used their military training to protect civil rights workers from assassination. In fact, many of the nonviolent marches and protests of the NAACP and CORE were made possible because of the armed security provided by the Deacons. Eventually, the FBI investigated and infiltrated the organization because of its willingness to engage in armed self-defense.[99]

In fact, the use and advocacy of violent resistance by the Deacons, Malcolm X, the Black Panther Party, Stokely Carmichael and SNCC, and others created a more serious threat to the power structure in that it forced facts on the public agenda and corporate media that contradicted the legitimizing narrative of the elite. And if the race narrative was shown to be a myth, then it logically followed that capitalism itself, upon which racism was grafted, was probably a myth as well, a point commonly raised by many groups of the CRBPM. As Chomsky, Max Weber, and others would say, illegitimate authority cannot tolerate any challenge to its legitimizing ideology. As such, the very act of revisiting racial history is a direct challenge to capitalism and its now neo-legitimizing myths of a nonviolent civil rights movement.

> "The experience of the Deacons," writes Lance Hill, "lays bare the myth of nonviolence, testifying to the crucial role of defensive violence in securing the law of the land." What Hill provocatively characterizes as the "myth of nonviolence" dovetails into a larger reconsideration of longstanding civil rights tropes that depict a world filled with polarities between pacifism and violence, nationalism and integration, and personified by divergent historical conceptions of Malcolm X and Martin Luther King Jr.[100]

In other words, militant direct action, defensive violence, and even revolutionary ideology were not separate from the CRBPM. On the contrary, it was interwoven between nonviolence practitioners, political reformers, and ultimately even social revolutionaries.

Little is mentioned today about Robert F. Williams[101] or the Black Panther Party during MLK celebrations, given the sanitization of the movement by the corporate media. Rob Williams exemplifies how a number of civil rights militants and revolutionaries expressed an overlapping ideology with the Black Power movement as it relates to violence and armed resistance. Early on, Williams saw violent self-defense as a complement to the nonviolent tactics of the civil rights movement in the South. However, he eventually rejected nonviolence altogether as ineffectual, focusing instead on resistance and an increasingly revolutionary internationalist ideology. Interestingly, although he advocated black separatism he connected US racism to the government and capitalism itself:

> In Havana and Beijing, he devised plans for an apocalyptic struggle with the white oppressor. In interviews with his first biographer Robert Carl Cohen in 1968, Williams insisted that the black revolutionary juggernaut would obliterate America. Black guerrillas would strike at the heart of the capitalist system, such as oil fields and pipelines. Using arson and sabotage, the black underground army would then destroy the nation's cities, and, eventually, the United States itself.[102]

The Black Panther Party, which was heavily influenced by Rob Williams, was an interesting organization in that it openly advocated and practiced armed resistance for self-defense and even revolution.[103] In California, members with legally registered guns and a copy of the Penal Code would shadow police patrols to ensure citizen rights were not violated.[104] Contrary to popular perception, the organization included and worked with white activists. The Black Panthers presented a direct and concrete threat to the institutional power structure because they did not simply dish out rhetoric. They engaged in societal education, offering free classes on economics and politics, ran one of the most successful testing programs for sickle-cell anemia, and became well known for their Free Breakfast for Children Program among other community based activities. They eventually came to be seen as a serious threat. FBI director J. Edgar Hoover declared that the group was a major "Marxist" threat to internal security—although they did not consider themselves Marxists.

Eventually, their popularity, radical Left ideology, and willingness to engage in armed resistance made them an investigation target of the FBI. The FBI through its COINTELPRO program engaged in infiltration, propaganda, surveillance, prosecutions, and a host of other illegal tactics. The FBI even engaged in assassinations of party members, the most famous being that of Fred Hampton, an effective organizer. Hampton was assassinated in his apartment by Chicago police on December 4, 1969, after FBI direct involvement.[105]

Dr. Martin Luther King is also presented in a non-threatening light these days, his radical arguments having been sanitized. Although an ardent proponent of nonviolent civil disobedience, he was not as docile as is commonly assumed. Instead, it was his class-conscious ideology rather than his actions which exhibited a well-articulated radicalism and anti-capitalism:

> Negroes in the United States read the history of labor and find it mirrors their own experience. We are confronted by powerful forces telling us to rely on the good will and understanding of those who profit by exploiting us. They are shocked that action organizations, sit-ins, civil disobedience and protests are becoming our everyday tools, just as strikes, demonstrations and union organization became yours to insure that bargaining power genuinely existed on both sides of the table. . . . That is why the labor-hater and labor-baiter is virtually always a twin-headed creature spewing anti-Negro epithets from one mouth and anti-labor propaganda from the other mouth.[106]

Other examples of his radical ideology can be found in speeches in which he stated that "black is beautiful," called for black political power in major US cities, condemned the Vietnam War while calling for global racial and class unity, referred to the US racist social structure as internal colonialism, and, toward the end of his life, echoed the rhetoric of Malcolm X and the Black Panther Party. Thus, he too was considered an ideological militant by the FBI, making him a major target of the COINTELPRO program.

Revolutionary Direct Action

Although there were many peaceful marches, the marchers were often heckled, abused, beaten, and even attacked and killed by police and white mobs alike. But the protesters themselves would often also respond with defensive violence when attacked. Such protests would turn into full-blown revolts—*riots* according to the corporate media—with casualties and attacks on private productive property of the elite via mass lootings. Examples of violent direct actions include the twenty-six Red Summer race riots of 1919;[107] Tulsa in 1921;[108] Philadelphia in 1964; Watts in 1965;[109] Detroit in 1967;[110] Newark in 1967;[111] and Plainfield, New Jersey in 1967.[112] For a comprehensive list, see Table 7.

Many of these revolts were sparked by events such as the killing of Dr. King or the beating of Marquette Fry and his mother by police prior to the Watts uprising. Their underlying cause, though, has always been a deep dissatisfaction, disenchantment, and overall alienation from capitalist racist society. Thus riots have been a direct reaction to racist capitalist oppression.[113] Contemporary Newark mayor Sharpe James blamed "the utter frustration that people had because of a hostile, brutal, and a non-responding government that ignored them and did not recognize their legitimate needs for the basics of life ... all denied a majority of people."[114] Furthermore, riots would lead in virtually all cases to mass lootings and destruction of private business property but not residences.[115] Therefore, this challenges the notion that these were indiscriminant riots. For example, Philadelphia, Watts, Detroit, Newark, and Plainfield were all characterized by widespread looting and thousands of burned stores.[116]

The Watts rebellion, in which tens of thousands participated, including 14,000 national guardsmen, provides a good example of how riots were more targeted than believed. The overall property damage was estimated at $45 million, which in today's dollars is over $296 million.[117] According to Theoharis:

> The riot was more targeted than public officials suggested. ... the Urban League's Watts project was unscathed, the only building not burned on the block. Some—but not all—white businesses in South L.A. were burned (such as the 4300 block of Central Avenue that restricted African Americans from renting business fronts and 37 of 40 savings and loans associations that charged higher interest rates in South L.A.); some—but not all—black establishments were spared. Aimed largely at commercial interests, most housing was untouched. Stan Myles, a black student at Cal-State Long Beach, explained that people were "not lawless"; community members volunteered to man street corners where traffic lights had gone out and drivers followed their lead. But it became easier to describe rioters as indiscriminate and criminal (although most arrested had no previous record) [many even had full-time jobs] than to grapple with the substance of the uprising. Chief Parker, for instance likened rioting blacks to "monkeys in a zoo."[118]

Interestingly, even art such as the 104 foot Watts Tower, a mosaic by Sabatino Rodia, was left unharmed. Tom Hayden, a white activist during the 1967 Newark rebellion, recalled "The first night, ... was primarily targeted looting. Black owned businesses as I recall were not looted."[119] He goes on to explain that "looters" mentioned specific business owners by name, complaining about specific grievances against them, e.g., rigged scales and cash registers. Black owned businesses put "soul brother" signs in their store fronts and were left alone, only to be targeted by the police and soldiers. Carol Glassman, another white activist in

Newark, recalled that "it was a little bit like a party. There was a lot of energy. People were talking and hanging out on the street."[120]

Seemingly this is an example of poor people engaging in opportunistic stealing, an image current in the media coverage at the time. This is probably true to an extent, but what underlies this action is the feeling of being disrespected, exploited, and impoverished. Ironically, this was the conclusion reached by the Kerner Commission of 1968 set up by Lyndon Johnson to examine the "riots" after Dr. King's assassination. Of course the commission did not explicitly blame racist capitalism, as this would have been unacceptable to the elite, opting instead to focus on racism and … inequality. Looting was thus an instinctual working-class or racial response to institutional exploitation and injustice. It is above all a direct attack on private business property and thus is revolutionary in its nature. The typical state response has been to deploy tens of thousands of police, national guards, federal troops, and mobs to restore government control with machine guns and heavy artillery.[121] Ironically, the state too would violate laws in its efforts to regain control.

Furthermore, many of these revolts were not ephemeral riots by youngsters detached from long histories of activism, as the Watts case demonstrates. "The notion that activism pre-Watts was strictly older generation and conciliatory is a troubling act of historical amnesia."[122] Instead, there was a long history of activism in Los Angeles prior to the revolt, centering on school desegregation.[123] And it was the passage of Proposition 14 which effectively re-permitted housing discrimination in California that sparked the revolt, rather than the police beating of Marquette Fry and his mother which was the pretext but not the cause.

Finally, there was also an economic aspect in the civil rights movement which supplemented the spontaneous revolts and lootings. Protesters engaged in economic boycotts of businesses and local governments. This was an effort to exact an economic toll on the elite in order to extract concessions. One of the first efforts to boycott segregationist bus companies was in 1953 by the UDL established in Baton Rouge, Louisiana. Later, the UDL became the model for the MIA which organized the more successful boycott of the Montgomery bus company, inflicting upon it a 65% drop in revenues.[124]

The most important lesson from the civil rights movement is that there was nothing handed willingly to blacks. They did not further their rights by asking power holders through nonviolence. Instead, blacks had to riot and engage in armed resistance, finally escalating in revolution. Nonviolence was only one strategy, which itself was often backed by arms and violence. Black people obtained their rights through violent revolutionary direct action, taking them back from the very institutions that had usurped them.[125] But this fact is deliberately ignored by the corporate mass media. Since the media are owned by and represent the interests of major corporations and the elite, they do not inform the public as to the effectiveness of violent direct resistance. Instead, they urge us to take our case to the courts they own using laws they made.

History shows us that the labor and civil rights movements sought liberation from alienating and enslaving capitalism. This is demonstrated by the common tactics used by these movements and the identical responses offered by the elite. For one, those in power make laws that criminalize any challenge to the structures underpinning the authority of the socioeconomic system. Consequently, both labor and the civil rights movement had to operate in defiance, and often outside of, existing legal parameters. The law did not provide rights. Rather, it acknowledged realities on the ground only after years of agitation and even rebellion as articulated by Rocker.[126] Today this means that the working class has a right, if not obligation, to operate in defiance of anti–working class legislation, which is the focus of the next chapter. This includes the right of engaging in sympathy or secondary strikes in support of workers in other establishments and industries—a right available to European workers and others around the world, resisting the permanent replacement of strikers, which is not allowed in European nations, abolishing any Patriot Act–style attacks on civil liberties, forming labor unions spontaneously despite prohibitive laws, as is done in other industrial nations, actively resisting arrests of strikers and demonstrators, including government employees violating the anti-labor Taylor Laws that prohibit public employees in New York State from going on strike; and simply refusing to comply with any other anti-working class laws.

Interestingly, as both movements have shown, when sufficiently threatened, capitalists and the state violated existing laws and violently suppressed mass protests. Troops and paramilitary groups often shot civilians to protect business property.[127] People were arrested and their homes were searched without warrants. Historically, governments and capitalists engaged in kangaroo-court prosecutions and executions, as with Joe Hill—who proclaimed at his execution *"Don't mourn for me. Organize!"* Other leaders, like Fred Hampton, were assassinated by government agencies or capitalist henchmen.

People's movements can be successful, however. As both movements demonstrated, *societal education* through independent media, schools, and art has been, and continues to be, important in terms of obtaining popular support, developing class consciousness beyond race or industry, and mobilizing people. Consequently, societal education increased the intensity of class conflict by challenging the dominant ideology, making critical education another form of revolutionary action.[128] To this end, it is imperative to form our own labor universities as was done in the past.[129]

In addition, media concentration and pro-capitalist bias have become a well-documented obstruction to objective information and democracy.[130] This is why it will be crucial for the new working-class movement to develop television stations, newspapers, radio stations, Internet media, and arts centers. As long as capitalists control the mass media their own interests will never be questioned, let alone challenged.

Ideology also matters, as does violent economic direct action, which has been revolutionary in that it complimented challenging the elites' political authority with challenges to their economic base as well. Shavar Jeffries, Newark Boys and Girls Clubs Board president, has stated, "I hope that we care that the future have another Newark rebellion because when I look at the vital signs of the city of Newark we need a rebellion, we need a revolution."[131] It is through militant direct actions that sudden change becomes possible. Although I do not advocate an immediate total overthrow of all social institutions, I support evolutionary but highly revolutionary changes in the relations of production and governance. One example offered in chapter two is corporate boards staffed exclusively by worker and community groups—something that in itself would require much bloodshed to accomplish.

Legislation has been repressive of the labor and civil rights movements, forcing them to operate outside of, and in direct opposition to, existing legal frameworks. Labor and civil rights have never been handed peacefully and voluntary changes in law never occurred in the name of progress and social justice. Instead, major legislative changes took place in response to a long history of agitation based on high levels of intense violent direct action and the threat of broader civil unrest. As demonstrated, when sufficiently threatened, capitalists and government violated existing laws and violently suppressed mass protests. This was a standard response every time the elite felt threatened. However, when the people defended themselves, they were eventually successful in obtaining their goals. The time has come for all working-class people to engage in a new movement of economic civil disobedience to liberate themselves from the yoke of capitalist boom-bust-bailout for the rich.

Notes

1. Aronowitz, 1992; Brecher, 1997; Mills, 1971 [1948].
2. Brecher, 1997.
3. Business unionism developed in the 1880s, when trade union leaders emphasized improvements in wages, hours, and working conditions, giving up on prior strategies of changing the political-economic system. Business unionism is literally operating the union as a business that sells labor. It stresses "pure and simple" goals and is associated with the co-optation of unions into the capitalist system rather than focusing on fundamental socioeconomic changes and opposition to the status quo.
4. Perlman, 1966.
5. London, 1989/90.
6. Thoreau, 1969 [1849].
7. Rocker, 1938.
8. In fact, most of the effective leaders and tactics of the labor movement have historically been branded as terrorism, vandalism, and many other negative characterizations in the mainstream press and by capitalists and politicians. There are many examples throughout time of judicial and extrajudicial executions and assassinations of labor leaders and organizers, and outlawing of labor and activist groups. Consequently, it is disingenuous to argue that radical labor tactics will be branded and suppressed as "terrorist" in modern times since this has always been the case whenever capital felt its interests truly threatened.
9. Brecher 1997; Graham and Gurr, 1969.
10. Brecher, 1997; Fording, 1997; Piven and Cloward, 1971.
11. Peck, 2002; Wolfson, 2003.
12. As cited in Guerin, 1970
13. Gramsci, 1971.
14. Rocker, 1938.
15. Altenbaugh, 1990; Shore, 1992; Teitelbaum, 1993; Weinstein, 1984.
16. Gramsci, 1971; Shore, 1992.
17. Krajnc, 2000; Lindsey, 1994.
18. Weinstein, 1984.
19. Krajnc, 2000.
20. Altenbaugh, 1990; Krajnc, 2000; Teitelbaum, 1993.
21. Greenway, 1970; Krajnc, 2000; Zaniello, 2003.
22. Montgomery, 1976: 116.
23. Greenway, 1970.
24. Krajnc, 2000; Montgomery, 1976.
25. Morgan, 1973; Young, 1999.

26. Montgomery, 1976: 123.
27. Brecher, 1997; Graham and Gurr, 1969.
28. Dacus, 1969; Foner, 2002; Stowell, 1999.
29. Krause, 1992; Wolff, 1965.
30. Carwardine, 1994; Hirsch, 2003; Lindsey, 1994.
31. Friedheim, 1964.
32. Fine, 1969; Linder, 1963.
33. Dacus, 1969; Foner, 2002; Stowell, 1999.
34. Lindsey, 1994.
35. Brecher, 1997; Montgomery, 1976.
36. Brecher, 1997.
37. Montgomery, 1976: 128.
38. Ibid., 124–125.
39. Cited in Wolff, 1965: 90.
40. Lindsey, 1994.
41. Ibid.
42. Montgomery, 1976: 128.
43. Cited in Friedheim, 1964: 132.
44. Cited in Brecher, 1997: 221.
45. Dacus, 1969; Foner, 2002.
46. Friedheim, 1964.
47. Cited in Friedheim, 1964: 111.
48. Roediger and Foner, 1989.
49. Ibid.
50. Ibid., 112.
51. Cited in Brecher, 1997: 54.
52. Brecher, 1997: 57.
53. Roediger and Foner, 1989: 138.
54. Montgomery, 1976: 126.
55. Roediger and Foner, 1989.
56. Brecher, 1997.
57. Roediger and Foner, 1989.
58. Ibid.
59. Roediger and Foner, 1989.
60. Cited in Alter, 2006: 3.
61. Ibid., 3–4.
62. Ibid., 4.
63. Perlman, 1939.
64. Alter, 2006: 4.
65. Fording, 1997: 23.

66. Alter, 2006; Asimakopoulos, 2000; Roediger and Foner, 1989.
67. Roediger and Foner, 1989.
68. Rocker, 1938.
69. Piven and Cloward, 1971.
70. Fording, 1997.
71. Hill, 2004; Strain, 2005; Tyson 1999; Umoja, 2002.
72. Bongiorno, 2007.
73. Peniel, 2006: 8.
74. Ibid., 22.
75. Ibid., 12.
76. The Counter Intelligence Program or COINTELPRO was a series of covert, and often illegal, projects conducted by the FBI, aimed at surveilling, infiltrating, discrediting, and disrupting domestic political organizations. Tactics included discrediting targets through psychological warfare, planting false reports in the media, smearing through forged letters, harassment, wrongful imprisonment, extralegal violence and assassination. Covert operations under COINTELPRO took place between 1956 and 1971. The FBI's stated motivation at the time was "protecting national security, preventing violence, and maintaining the existing social and political order." FBI records show that 85% of COINTELPRO resources targeted groups and individuals that the FBI deemed "subversive," including communist and socialist organizations; organizations and individuals associated with the civil rights movement, including Dr. Martin Luther King, Jr. and others associated with the Southern Christian Leadership Conference, the National Association for the Advancement of Colored People, and the Congress of Racial Equality and other civil rights organizations; black nationalist groups; the American Indian Movement; a broad range of organizations labeled "New Left," including Students for a Democratic Society and Weatherman; almost all groups protesting the Vietnam War, as well as individual student demonstrators with no group affiliation; the National Lawyers Guild; organizations and individuals associated with the women's rights movement; nationalist groups such as those seeking independence for Puerto Rico and a united Ireland; and additional notable Americans, such as Dr. Albert Einstein.
77. Churchill and Wall, 2002.
78. Klarman, 2004.
79. Malcolm X, 1965: 53.
80. Bongiorno, 2007.
81. Meier and Rudwick, 1975.

82. Stoper, 1989; Zinn, 2002.
83. Morris, 1984.
84. Garrow, 1989.
85. Krajnc, 2000.
86. Glen, 1996.
87. Krajnc, 2000.
88. Smethurst, 2005.
89. Bongiorno, 2007.
90. Ogbar, 2004.
91. Hill, 2004.
92. Tyson, 1999.
93. Black Capitalism is a movement among blacks to build wealth through the ownership and development of businesses.
94. Klarman, 2004.
95. Malcolm X, 1965: 26.
96. Ibid., 32.
97. Marx and Engels, 1978 [1848]: 500.
98. Carmichael, 1965: 54–60.
99. Hill, 2004.
100. Peniel, 2006: 14.
101. Tyson, 1999.
102. Wendt, 2006: 163–64.
103. Abu-Jamal, 2004.
104. Wendt, 2006.
105. Abu-Jamal, 2004.
106. King, 1991: 202–03.
107. Tuttle, 1996.
108. Madigan, 2001.
109. Boesel and Rossi, 1971; Rossi, 1973.
110. Ibid.
111. Ibid.
112. Ibid.
113. Kerner Commission, 1968.
114. Cited in Bongiorno, 2007.
115. Rossi, 1973.
116. Boesel and Rossi, 1971; Rossi, 1973.
117. Author's calculations, http://www.measuringworth.com/index.html.
118. Theoharis, 2006: 50.
119. Cited in Bongiorno, 2007.
120. Ibid.

121. Brecher, 1997; Graham and Gurr, 1969.
122. Theoharis, 2006: 45.
123. Ibid.
124. Garrow, 1989; Krajnc, 2000; Morris, 1984.
125. Fording, 1997.
126. Rocker, 1938.
127. Brecher 1997; Graham and Gurr, 1969.
128. Macrine et al., 2009.
129. Altenbaugh, 1990; Teitelbaum, 1993.
130. Chomsky, 1994, 2002; Greenwald, 2004.
131. Cited in Bongiorno, 2007.

4

Direct Action: Loot the Rich

"Isn't it hypocritical for Lyndon [president Johnson] to talk about how you can't accomplish anything by looting."
Stokely Carmichael

The working class has been defeated on a global scale while the remnants of the Western European welfare state wither away as Labor and Conservative governments—Democrats and Republicans in the United States—take turns governing their de facto corporate states. Now, declining unionization rates and increasing globalization are accelerating the concentration of wealth by the hyper rich. Poverty has been on the rise as the overall living standards of the working-class population have been steadily deteriorating over the past forty years.[1] Increasingly, workers are left without health care or other basic services while the feminization of poverty, the working poor, and contingent employment have been normalized. Consumer debt and foreclosures have been at record highs for years, surpassed perhaps by people's disillusionment with the "American Nightmare." Welcome to the McDonaldized world where you can super-size anything but your Walmart wage. So, what is labor to do in the face of an unresponsive union leadership, globalization, downsizings into less-than-subsistence service jobs, and unilateral suspension of collective bargaining itself in 2011 by states like Wisconsin? Vote for the Barack Obamas of America who wine and dine with the vassals of corporate power? No.

Unfortunately, as history suggests, reliance on the political process is a failed strategy. For example, the minimum wage would bring a full-time employee close to the federal poverty line in the militant 1960s whereas in 2004 it was just 56% of the poverty level.[2] In 1969 the Gini ratio of inequality for households was 0.391 vs. 0.463 in 2007.[3] The poverty rate for families in 1969 was 9.7% vs. 10.3% in 2008.[4] The unemployment rate in 1969 was 3.5% vs. 10.1% in October of 2009.[5] Unionization rates declined from around 36% in the 1940s to under 7% currently. Globalization has accelerated these trends. Meanwhile, the share of aggregate household income received by the top 5% jumped to 21.5% in 2008 vs. 16.6% in 1969.[6] All this has happened under what is supposedly a democratic regime.

Unions and activist groups need to engage the working class and cultivate a movement from below. The only people who can help workers are themselves—through class consciousness and organized resistance to capitalism—not politicians or political parties. Unions need to capture workers' imaginations and awaken them from their slumber, not through empty rhetoric and tidy demonstrations but through radical actions with real risks and real outcomes. The working class needs to engage in a new radical movement of economic civil disobedience detached from the existing institutional and legal frameworks through workers' organizations which are not covered by the now anti-labor National Labor Relations Board (NLRB).[7] As chapter three demonstrated, this new movement should be modeled on the US civil rights and labor movements of the past. These movements are appropriate models because they were effective due to their radical nature. Specifically, they challenged existing institutional frameworks through militant ideology and societal education (which increased the intensity of class conflict) and civil disobedience coupled with violent resistance (which hasten change).

The mass movement literature is slowly suggesting that violent direct action does have an impact on the elite. In the past, it has been found that welfare spending increases in response to civil unrest in order to pacify the poor.[8] In addition violence has been more effective when the protest group had access to or wields electoral power. More recent studies, using a pooled time-series model, confirm that violence is more effective than conventional means in obtaining concessions.[9] Accordingly, the effectiveness of violence, including looting, rock throwing, beatings, vandalism, arson, etc., depends on four factors. These are the size of the insurgent group, its relationship with broader society, the presence of democratic institutions, and the insurgent group's access to these institutions.[10]

Today, such conditions for successful use of violent civil disobedience are present for labor. Thus, we need a new form of militant direct economic civil disobedience capable of exacting significant financial blows to capitalism. Direct action must be at an increased level of actual and threatened use of violence to increase the effectiveness of achieving working-class goals. However, most mainstream academics, activists, and labor leaders oppose such action that would seriously hurt, cripple, or even bankrupt corporations. It is as if labor has become a parasitic organism that can only live off corporations.[11] This predicament reveals the current general lack of class consciousness. In addition, when writers do suggest that labor engage in civil disobedience they only propose nonviolent actions such as protest marches. For disobedience to be an effective tool of change the one being harmed must not be the protester but the protested. This is difficult to achieve with nonviolence alone. Instead, citizens must engage in actions that have a direct, immediate, significant, and quantifiable impact on the ruling class. Labor will obtain significant gains only when the elite realize that their authority and financial interests are directly threatened.

As chapter one has shown, globalization unfortunately has privileged multinational corporations relative to a national workforce, making it difficult to financially affect them with localized or even national level strikes alone. The primary reason is that multinational corporations can easily shift production to a number of their global plants.[12] Therefore localized strikes have become an ineffective means of inflicting financial costs upon corporations, thanks to America's anti-labor laws. This is why we need to find additional means through which to inflict a financial toll on anti-labor capital, such as Walmart, until that long-term revolution materializes. To achieve this, labor must be re-radicalized and broaden direct action into new socioeconomic spheres at significantly higher levels of conflict than at present.

Proposed direct actions include disobedience of restrictive labor laws and institutions, e.g., Taylor Laws, Taft-Hartley, the NLRB; violent resistance to reactionary state violence; mass organized lootings, e.g., of corporate stores, distribution warehouses, and financial institutions; high-stakes tax resistance; subversive financial actions; and establishment of counter-institutions. These strategies are suggested as a supplement to traditional work actions which are also encouraged at far higher levels of militancy, such as mass and sympathy strikes (perhaps the United States could see its first national strike); work slowdowns; sabotage; militant picket lines; retail, plant, or office occupations; destruction of corporate property; etc. These actions attack the system at its core.

DISOBEYING THE LAW

Those trying to subvert militant resistance to an ideology of inequality and domination often quote the rule of law. But what if the legal framework is part of the problem to begin with? Once it was illegal to form a union, to strike, or for women and blacks to vote. These laws have been mostly conceived, written, promoted, and voted in by capitalist institutions and their representatives.[13] Now we need to continue the civil rights and labor struggles through an economic civil disobedience movement willing to disobey anti-working class legislation in general.

Labor law upholds capitalism by making many important working-class tactics illegal. For example, the Taft-Hartley Act of 1947 forbids secondary or sympathy strikes and boycotts. This greatly reduces the economic impact of strikes and working-class solidarity across firms and industries. The reorganization of the NLRB has made it very cumbersome to legally establish a union, therefore limiting union growth—a distinctively American practice. Also, *NLRB v. Mackay Radio & Telegraph* (1938) is used to permanently replace striking workers with strike breakers, another American practice. New York State's Taylor Law denies public employees the right to strike, with other states now using budget deficits as a pretext to suspend collective bargaining with public employees altogether. Finally, because labor contracts include a no-strike clause, workers are not allowed to strike for the duration of the contract. Worse, labor contracts routinely require workers with workplace grievances, some life-threatening, to continue working under those conditions until the grievance is formally resolved. Unfortunately, this can take years and it is commonplace for union officials to bargain away dozens of grievances as negotiating chips in exchange for other gains deemed important by the union. Labor law in America is so restrictive that many have argued that workers would be better off without it.[14]

Another broader example of anti-working class legislation is the tax code which is highly regressive in the United States compared with significantly progressive tax codes in other industrialized nations. Worse, our legislation includes massive subsidies to large corporations, commonly referred to as *wealthfare*. In addition, the criminal code provides for far more lenient punishments and sentencing guidelines for white-collar and corporate crime. As of 2011 no one has been charged or jailed for their role in the systemic financial fraud that devastated the global economy in 2008.

But when a group is oppressed by law it has the right to actively resist.[15] For example, the most significant organizing victories in recent years were won by hospital and farm workers who are not covered by the NLRB and by public employees who engaged in illegal strikes resulting in jailings of their leadership.[16] Thus, workers and the poor need to reject such legal frameworks whose compliance is based on only two factors: false class consciousness and state violence. When the first fails through education and when vested interests of the elite are challenged, the state is quick to use violence.

The law permits revolving doors between government and corporate office despite clear conflicts of interest; the use of bankruptcy law to break unions, cut wages, and lay-off thousands; the use of prison labor; subsidies to wealthy corporations; the transfer of billions of public dollars to corporations; corporate looting of pensions; massive corporate tax breaks, evasion, and loopholes. What the law does not permit is sympathy strikes, a simplified unionization process, the prohibition of strike breakers, and the universal right to strike.

Tax Resistance

Economic civil disobedience must target the state as the political power base of capitalists. State violence is routinely used to protect elite interests when these are threatened. This makes the state a legitimate target for direct action. Ideally, the working class should try to take peaceful control of the state which is theoretically possible, given the basic democratic structure of the United States. This, though, is unlikely, given America's winner-take-all electoral system[17] and the absence of a major working-class political party,[18] not to mention media concentration in elite hands. Therefore, an immediate strategy should focus on depriving the state of financial resources in order to undermine its ability to engage in violence. After all, the state never prioritizes social expenditures anyway. This can be done by denying it tax revenues through various kinds of tax resistance strategies. Iraq and Afghanistan for example, have cost us over one trillion dollars—not counting the cost in human lives—with yet more billions to come.[19] Compare that to the $6.8 billion spent on Head Start in 2005[20] or the fact that the United States is the only industrialized nation without a free comprehensive national healthcare system. Tax resistance, though, must be at much higher levels than that of groups which usually practice it. How can this be done and is it moral? To answer this let's see what corporations and the wealthy do so that we may learn from *them*.

Where a corporation is based makes a difference on how it is taxed. Thus, many of the largest US companies have moved, incorporating themselves in offshore tax havens, usually Antigua, Bermuda, or the Cayman Islands. The company headquarters does not physically move. It is all done on paper, using a post office box located in one of those nations. Tyco International did it, saving $400 million, as did companies like PricewaterhouseCoopers and Arthur Andersen.[21] As a result, between 1983 and 1999 America's top 10,000 corporations saw a 735% increase in profits thanks to offshore incorporation.[22] Also, companies can open offshore bank accounts again protecting funds from US taxation. It is estimated that American companies have upwards of $3 trillion deposited in these accounts.[23]

Transnationals also reduce their tax bills through "transfer pricing." A company sells goods or services to itself at very high prices in high-tax nations and very low prices in low-tax nations, thus transferring profits to the low- or no-tax nations. For example, one company bought from its Brazilian subsidiary a bottle of salad dressing for $720 while another sold a missile launcher to its Israeli subsidiary for $22.[24] As a result of these tax strategies, loopholes, tax breaks, special exemptions, etc. corporations in the United States account for 15% of the federal government's general revenues, down from about 31% in the 1950s.[25]

The richest 1% of Americans own about half of all stock while the bottom 80% own only 4.1%.[26] The rich, though, do not benefit from these corporate tax strategies only through their stock holdings. It is not enough that companies like Microsoft made $12.3 billion in 1999 but paid nothing in taxes, that WorldCom paid nothing on $15.5 billion in profits, and General Electric has been paying effectively an 11.5% tax bill.[27] The rich avoid paying income taxes as well. For example, according to the IRS, 101 millionaires paid nothing in income taxes.[28] On top of that, all administrations cut taxes for the rich to one degree or another. George W. Bush's massive tax cuts benefited almost entirely the highest earning households. In addition to income taxes, there is the regressive nature of many types of taxes, such as the social security tax which is levied only on the first $87,000 of income. Thus, billionaires pay social security tax only on their first $87,000 of income, whereas a school teacher earning less than $50,000 has her entire income taxed.

Organized Lootings

Economic civil disobedience must directly target the corporation as the economic power base of the elite. It is through the corporation that the upper class raises funds with which to rig the political-legislative process via lobbying, campaign financing, and corruption.[29] Corporate earnings also finance the mass media, whose primary goals are to increase consumption and create the illusion of democracy while shaping public opinion. In addition, the elite use their ownership of the means of production to reap profits by exploiting workers through low wages, temporary and part-time work, and little to no benefits. Today wages are not even sufficient to cover the cost of "necessary labor."[30] Workers have no health care or other basic benefits required for a healthy family life and poverty wages are not adequate for the working class to raise children and reproduce itself.

The riots of 1992 in Los Angeles and the civil rights and old labor movement era were characterized by massive looting and anger.[31] At their core these events were a revolt against the unfairness of the system. People were angry and frustrated, lashing out against the power holders and attacking their private property. What is needed today is a well-organized plan of Robin Hood–style mass lootings. For example, in the summer of 2008, Greek anarchists engaged in direct action against price inflation of basic foods. They developed a program of looting food from large supermarkets, giving it away for free at farmers' markets to the old and needy. Many a grandmother could be seen on Greek television thanking the young anarchists for their assistance, to the dismay of frustrated corporate media reporters. Now people must take the lead from the Greek anarchists and organize to loot major retailers for as long as they refuse to become socially responsible employers. This should be done with organized stormings of stores using designated guards and coordinators warning employees and customers not to interfere. This would bring direct action to the ruling classes' doorsteps, generating broader news coverage. Lootings should not target small mom-and-pop businesses. What should be targeted, though, in addition to corporate retailers, are the corporations producing these products. For example, companies have their own warehouses from which they distribute products to retail outlets. These distribution centers must be targeted as well. Lastly, the strength of this tactic is that participants can conceal their identity to avoid prosecution. Let the exploited expropriate the exploiters.

The common threads among mass strikes like the Seattle General Strike of 1919 are a challenge to existing authorities, workers' tendency to direct themselves, and development of worker solidarity—in other words, libertarian socialism.[32] Since workers do not own the means of production, mass strikes aim toward the control of production. This means replacing society's power holders, making mass strikes a revolutionary process. It is suggested that working-class people and unions also focus on the other side of the production equation which is output. Thus, self-management and expropriation of private productive property should be supplemented with efforts to expropriate outputs as with organized lootings. Is this a new idea? No. Looting has been practiced for a very long time (historically think of colonialism and neocolonialism) and at a far greater cost by corporations themselves.

To this day corporations routinely loot the poor through poverty-level wages, no benefits, and prison labor. They loot the Treasury via tax strategies that deprive government of revenue. Corporations also loot government coffers through subsidies, public handouts, military waste, and fraud. The only difference with the looting proposed here is that corporate looting is legal. Matters could hardly be otherwise. Corporations simply enact legislation that they purchased using politicians that go through the revolving door between corporate and government executive positions.

One of the greatest lootings of the poor occurred in 2008–2009 when government bailed out the hyper rich. By the summer of 2009, $787 billion in stimulus spending had been approved by the federal government alone after it spent over $700 billion for the Troubled Asset Relief Program (TARP) and billions more for bailing specific corporations. All this occurred with trillions more in additional commitments by the US government. These bailouts represent the greatest wealth transfer of our times from everyone to the hyper rich, for a number of reasons.

As we have seen, the rich and corporations pay no taxes. To the contrary, they get subsidies which are also taxpayer derived. Everyone else pays taxes, including income, property, and, the most regressive of them all, sales (consumption) taxes, in addition to indirect taxes such as tolls and speeding tickets. Worse yet, these tax revenues are nowhere near sufficient to finance the military-industrial complex, corporate subsidies, bailouts, and more such goodies for the masters of society. As a result, historic national deficits are generated which also benefit the rich in many ways. For one, when government runs deficits it finances them through borrowing via the issuance of financial instruments such as Treasury bills. Essentially, these are IOUs. But those who purchase the overwhelming amount of these securities are not your typical American. Rather it is the (international) rich, either directly or indirectly, e.g., through hedge funds, and therefore it is they who benefit from the rate of return, the interest, on this debt which is paid by, yes, the taxpayer.

When bubbles burst, be they in technologies as in the 1990s or housing more recently, the rich benefit yet again. Instead of cutting wealthfare, the government slashes social services that benefit the poor. After all, corporations are "too big to fail" compared to your household. The budget ax falls instead on educational spending, health-care programs, and child welfare services. This has the effect of further immiserating the working class and beating it into submission through insecurity and want. To paraphrase George Orwell from *1984*, a hierarchy of society is only possible on the basis of poverty and ignorance. Consequently, the poor pay for all and get nothing in return. This makes deficits stolen wealth from the public. Had government taxed the rich and corporations at appropriate levels instead of subsidizing them there would be no deficit and thus no cuts in social programs. Consequently there are two fundamental solutions. First, tax both the income and wealth of the elite as need be to sustain a humane society. Unfortunately, since the elite are the judiciary, legislature, and executive, given their total domination of society this seems improbable. The other solution is for everyone else to engage in economic civil disobedience, e.g., by refusing to pay taxes, calling them instead what they really are: forced financial servitude for the benefit of the elite. Post-industrial peasants, take-up your pitchforks![33]

In addition to the epic bailout of 2009, corporations in America receive approximately $815 billion a year in wealthfare from the federal government alone compared to $193 billion for welfare for the poor—including food stamps, housing assistance, temporary aid to needy families, legal services, low-income energy assistance, Head Start, and WIC.[34] Corporate wealthfare includes $224 billion in military waste and fraud. For the years 1985 to 1995 the Pentagon does not know what happened to $28 billion of its own money—you know, like when you lose your pocket change in the couch cushions. Contractors routinely overcharge the Pentagon, e.g., McDonnell Douglas sold metal nuts worth less than a dollar to the navy for $2,043 each. Pentagon audits found Halliburton had over $1.422 billion in questionable costs.[35] Appearing before a congressional panel in 2003, a twenty-year veteran for military procurement said it was "the most blatant and improper contract abuse I have witnessed during the course of my professional career."[36] In addition, the top ten weapons contractors have all admitted or been convicted of fraud yet continue to do business with the government. The only company ever suspended was GE, the worst offender. The suspension lasted five days.[37]

Furthermore, there are the massive subsidies to logging, mining, nuclear, aviation, agribusiness, and other companies. For example, 43% of Archer Daniels Midland (a multinational agribusiness) profits come from subsidized products.[38] On top of that we have a giving away of public resources to corporations or selling them far below market value. Media companies, including GE, owner of NBC,[39] and Disney, owner of ABC, are given public airwaves, valued at over $14 billion a year, for free provided they serve the public interests. The problem: "The definition of public interests has become so loose today that the chair of the FCC

(Federal Communications Commission) says that he has no idea what it is."[40]

Compare all this to the annual cost of shoplifting by consumers, estimated at $10 billion, and employee theft at $15.1 billion.[41] Bad checks, cash shortages, and credit card charge-backs altogether amount to about 1% of annual retailer sales.[42] Of course, if individuals are convicted of such offenses they could go to jail, but not corporations for their looting activities. How do companies get away with their theft? The answer is institutionalized corruption.

For one, these corporations make massive political contributions, including outright bribes. What is more disturbing, because it is legal, is the direct staffing of key government positions with corporate executives despite clear conflicts of interest.[43] In fact, corporate executives are often put in governmental positions responsible for the policing of the very industries they came from. For example, former vice president Dick Cheney, who orchestrated the Iraq war, was Halliburton's CEO. Halliburton received the largest Iraq military contract, estimated at over $7 billion, without a bidding process (which is mandated for federal contracts within the US) and then engaged in unsubstantiated charges and overcharging.

Corporate McPoliticians are not scholars capable of drafting their own legislation nor do they draft policy in the public interest. The think tanks and policy institutes from which these McPoliticians obtain legislation and advice are dominated through staffing and financing by the same corporate elite who shape public policy.[44] This is achieved by their de facto monopolization of major think tanks, foundations, and advisory groups through their deep funding and staffing. For example, the Council on Foreign Relations, the Conference Board, etc., are major policy formation groups with deep ties to government and mostly dominated by corporate executives and members of the upper class.[45]

Financial Resistance

Economic civil disobedience must target financial institutions which are the financial power base of capitalists. Major banks and corporations use their financial power to legally and illegally defraud people and the public treasury alike. Under-funding or looting pension funds and using Chapter 11 bankruptcy to break unions are a good example of such legalized financial fraud. Corporations and the wealthy, though, also engage in outright theft. The list of frauds, theft, conspiracy, and financial collapse is staggering. The king of fraud is undoubtedly Enron, once the nineteenth largest US corporation under CEO and long-time Bush friend

Ken Lay.[46] Enron's top management engaged in systemic company-wide fraud to hide losses. One strategy was to move losses to offshore companies with names that were indicative of management's unlimited hubris and "master of the universe" mindset. For example, one such straw company was named M. Yass.[47] Another way Enron made money was through conspiring with power plants to limit electrical supply, effectively manufacturing the California energy crisis.[48] The crises drove up the cost of electricity for citizens and profits for Enron while costing the state of California $6 billion in overcharges.[49] When the Enron con game was about to implode, the company raided employees' pension funds.[50]

Enron, however, was assisted in its looting of employee pensions, the public, and the Treasury by major financial institutions such as Citigroup, Merrill Lynch, and J.P. Morgan Chase, and the accounting firm Arthur Andersen, which were fully aware of what was really going on.[51] Not surprisingly, these were the same financial companies responsible for the collapse of 2008 just a few years later. Back then, these companies conspired with Enron out of greed for their lucrative fees or what we would call bribes. J.P. Morgan Chase, in a series of lawsuits and investigations, agreed to pay back $3.3 billion. Arthur Andersen was convicted of obstruction of justice (later overturned by the Supreme Court) and is now virtually debunked. Two Merrill Lynch executives were also convicted of fraud for their enabling role in the Enron scam.[52]

Other major frauds that we know of include one by Tyco's Dennis Kozlowski (CEO) and Mark Swartz (CFO) who looted more than $600 million and were convicted of grand larceny, falsifying business records, securities fraud, and conspiracy.[53] WorldCom (later MCI) CEO Bernard Ebbers was convicted of an $11 billion accounting fraud and agreed to divest looted personal assets worth more than $45 million.[54] Adelphia founder John Rigas (CEO) and son Timothy (CFO) agreed to forfeit their looted personal assets valued at over $1.5 billion and were convicted of conspiracy, bank fraud, securities fraud, and looting the company and its investors.[55] Global Crossing's founder and chairman Gary Winnick, together with top management, falsified financial documents and agreed to repay $19.5 million, while Citigroup agreed to pay $75 million for its role in the collapse.[56]

More recently, Wall Street, with the assistance of the Federal Reserve, inflated the housing market and constructed the infamous securitized mortgage investments. They also conjured up the credit default swaps (derivatives), a financial instrument few claim to understand even among experts, due to their complex nature. None other than the "Oracle of Omaha," financier Warren Buffett, has described these instruments as "financial weapons of mass destruction."[57] These risky insurance policy gambles grew into an unregulated market valued into the trillions of dollars prior to the financial meltdown of 2008. When the collapse finally came, instead of letting the free market deal with it, all the guilty players, such as American International Group (AIG) and Goldman Sachs, lined up and got epic billion-dollar bailouts from their golf buddies whose turn it was at the time to double as government executives, like Treasury Secretary Henry Paulson, former Goldman Sachs CEO. Furthermore, it has been revealed that far more conversations took place than originally disclosed, raising ethics questions, between Paulson and Lloyd Blankfein, Goldman's CEO, compared with any other executives of the institutions involved.[58] This was the same week that rival Lehman Brothers was allowed to collapse while AIG, closely connected to Goldman Sachs, was rescued with over $85 billion of our tax dollars. Not to worry, though, if you are another Wall Street corporation. Within weeks they received the TARP at the tune of $700 billion, with additional trillions in federal guarantees, plus $9 trillion in zero-interest loans from the Federal Reserve that were disclosed only because of an act of congress![59] Yet the United States has been and is the only industrialized nation without a guaranteed national health-care system. For that congress needs many more centuries of research and debate before acting, unlike for the more important TARP funds.

But why target with direct action financial institutions such as banks in addition to the corporations that have engaged in financial abuses? The top financial institutions interlock with the boards of directors of America's top corporations.[60] As such, banks coordinate and facilitate capitalist interests.[61] For example, banks are the major stock voters in over 122 of the largest US corporations.[62] This reduces competition among corporations, creates unified business and political agendas, and formulates a highly self-conscious corporate-capitalist class.[63]

Second, these financial institutions usually issue the credit cards of major retailers and other businesses. Thus, if there is a work action, e.g., at a major retailer, why not financially target its credit card issuer or creditors in general? This is another way of forcing capitalists to put pressure on other capitalists that are targeted by worker action to settle the dispute as with a sympathy strike. Third, these financial institutions are also responsible for scams and frauds against the credit card users themselves. There is ample data on unreasonable late fees and other fees, usury interest rates, bait-and-switch offers, and predatory practices that blatantly defraud consumers and especially working-class minorities.[64]

Fourth, historically and with government assistance, as with the racist Fannie Mae programs of the 1960s, banks engaged in "redlining" denying people of color and poor people mortgages and other financial services. They still charge higher interest rates and offer worse terms to those communities compared to white and middle-class ones. Worse, many banks do not even locate branches in poor communities, leading to the mushrooming of check-cashing businesses that charge exorbitant amounts for services that are normally free, e.g., cashing a payroll check. Furthermore, it was banks, together with Wall Street financial institutions, that enabled the housing bubble with fraudulent lending practices. These included "NINJA" loans, subprime loans issued to borrowers with No Income, No Job, (and) no Assets, and no-money-down mortgages (compared to the traditional 20%), which dramatically ballooned in two to three years out of the borrowers reach. These institutions targeted people they knew could never repay the loans because, instead of holding on to them, banks would "securitize" and sell them to other institutions, earn fees from originating and reselling the loans, and had no reason to worry if the loans went bad since they had been resold.

Obviously, working-class people have neither the skill nor access to commit frauds of such epic proportions. Some suggested strategies, though, include deliberate worker-organized credit card frauds. Why target credit card companies with direct action? Who owns and issues credit cards: the same major financial institutions that enabled major corporate fraud at Enron, WorldCom, etc., and the collapse of 2008. For example, over 72% of the credit card market is dominated by the top five credit card companies including Citigroup and J.P. Morgan Chase.[65] Finally, as the representatives of financial capital, banks should also be targeted with organized lootings. The working class could storm the vaults of bank branches distributing the cash to the needy and charitable organizations. Long live Robin Hood!

The working class should also take advantage of bankruptcy laws. It's time for workers to use the same laws to their benefit. For example, there are still many people who consider it a matter of honor to avoid bankruptcy. Unions and other organizations should actively encourage and help people file for bankruptcy. Of course, bankruptcy laws for corporations differ from those for consumers, with the latter changed to be more restrictive. People should also refuse to make student loan, car, mortgage, and other loan payments when downsized, on strike, or victims of poverty wages with no benefits. And if the repo man comes for the house or car, let communities say no. In fact, the Association of Community Organizations for Reform Now (ACORN) organized direct actions to resist evictions of families being foreclosed, which was the true reason for the attacks on the organization by conservatives, government, and the media.[66] Why not have a "borrowers' revolt" as the modern equivalent of Shays' Rebellion and the 1830s land-rent revolts? Organize community action committees (mobs), as did farmers during the Great Depression, to chase away and prevent auctions of foreclosed homes, repossessed cars, or anything else.

Electronic Resistance

Viral direct action and electronic civil disobedience could also be used by organized workers against corporations and elite interests generally. The idea can be traced back to at least the mid-1990s by groups such as the Critical Art Ensemble. This was a way to counter "the de-centralized and de-territorialized nature of contemporary capitalism, particularly financial capital."[67] Examples would include virus attacks, hijacking websites, shutting down corporate computer systems through denial-of-service attacks, etc. Why not hijack Walmart's website and advertise its labor abuses? This would deprive these corporations of sales, inform the public, and probably get the attention of the mass media, spreading the message as was done with deliberate actions by the civil rights movement. For example, in 1998 a pro-Zapatista group, the Electronic Disturbance Theater, flooded the Mexican president's website with a list of people killed in Acteal. This was done with FloodNet software that the group developed for such electronic direct actions.[68]

Another example of electronic civil disobedience includes WikiLeaks and its founder, Julian Assange. The organization was established in 2006, its primary mission being the release of private, classified, mostly state documents into the public domain. In 2010 it garnered international attention and the collective wrath of world governments especially the United States, for leaking highly sensitive, embarrassing, and even shocking diplomatic cables on its website. Here it was governments who attacked the organization's website to prevent it from further exposing their corruption.

So why not hack into secret company files and learn what the company's financial books really look like? Gathering of strategic information is done daily by the FBI and CIA against us and other governments, by corporations against each other, through corporate espionage, and the public with computer "cookies" which are legal practice. Electronic civil disobedience would help the working-class share resources, organize, and promote knowledge. It also provides a greater opportunity for political involvement to those who are disenchanted by the available political options and structure.[69]

The value of social media and the ability to communicate in general was demonstrated in the revolts of 2011. Using the Internet and social media, e.g., Facebook and Twitter, the people of Tunisia were able to organize a seemingly spontaneous organic revolution to oust their dictatorial government. News of the successful revolution reached Egypt, Yemen, and other Middle Eastern dictatorships, bringing with it additional revolts in those nations. All of this was made possible by telecommunications that could not be controlled by government. In fact, this led to a historic first for the Internet. On Friday, January 28, 2011, Egyptian authorities effectively shut down the Internet for the entire country, recognizing its organizational value for the opposition, to little avail, though.

Counter-Institutions

It is not enough to take back from the rich what is rightfully ours, we also need to learn how to manage our own affairs. This is what power fears most: what would happen should the people learn to manage their own administrative and productive affairs without bosses? This is why the working class needs to establish its own counter-institutions as an additional long-term form of resistance advocated by participatory economics strategies.[70] To demonstrate, I offer the nonprofit think tank Transformative Studies Institute (TSI) as an example. The institute was born out of what a labor arbitrator termed an "arbitrary and capricious" firing: I was fired for activist work but primarily for questioning administrative authority and illicit practices. Other educators and I decided that the problem lay with the power elite who have been taking over the last bastions of free thought and therefore resistance to their domination, academia. The corporatization of the university is one means through which the power elite tighten their grip on the reproduction of the dominant ideology as we have seen in previous chapters.

So, my friends, colleagues, and I decided to establish a legally recognized counter-institution, educational in nature, in the form of a nonprofit. This way we are reclaiming legitimacy for our progressive ideology while counterbalancing the impact of corporate universities. First, it is quickly evident by looking at our affiliated people that TSI is quite capable of producing some impressively high-quality radical counter ideology. We pride ourselves for recruiting faculty who have earned their wings by being fired from at least one college or banned by a country, as our friend Steve Best, who is banned from the United Kingdom for advocating animal liberation. We support the marginalized, the exploited, the terminated, the unemployable.

Second, as a nonprofit institution we operate unconstrained by University, Inc. We offer various educational programs and services to the working class, e.g., we run a prisoner education program, "Education Through Bars." TSI is also in the process of establishing itself as an accredited graduate school to further engage in societal education. Third, we recognize the value of independent media and founded *Theory in Action*, our own peer-reviewed journal, as well as the online Transformative Radio. We initiated our own book press in collaboration with like-minded publishing houses, and a speakers' bureau.

We collaborate with activists and other progressive nonprofits to support those who resist daily: the graduate teaching assistant who tries to organize colleagues or college janitors, the environmentalist fighting a polluting factory in the community, the mother who demands that Newark, provide equal quality public education for her children, and the father who fights his HMO to authorize the procedure that will save his child's life.

We have learned skills that we would otherwise never have learned, and have found refuge from our alienating "assembly-line" teaching. In short, we won a sense of freedom. Others must also reclaim their social institutions even if it means leaving behind the decadent existing ones.

Finally, the working class needs to relearn old yet effective tactics. Mass strikes have virtually disappeared in America while sympathy strikes have been outlawed. The time has come for America's first-ever national strike as is done routinely in European countries and other nations around the world. Sympathy strikes should also become an ingrown habit of all workers, even at the cost of arrest. If we all strike, either in sympathy or in violation of strike laws, as with public employees, what will they do? Arrest us all? Fire us all? It is only with a terrorized and fractured working class that they can arrest or fire the lone-dog striker. No, shut down the nation for a week and see what happens.

As for the perverse allowance of strike breakers and permanent replacements, workers need to kindly inform them that they are being used to break a work action by their brothers and sisters and ask them to join the strike instead or leave. In the past, workers turned violent against willing strike breakers, and the state and corporate thugs that guarded them.[71] This created fear of a severe beating, making these people think twice before abusing another worker or community.

Furthermore, as a worker, do not be afraid to sabotage these corporations as long as they do not accept legitimate demands. Occupy their plants, offices, and retail outlets. Destroy all of their private corporate property but without the taking or harming of life. If the plant is going to close or relocate in China for cheap labor what do you have to lose? You are going to be out of a job anyway.

"But they will send the police to break us up!" Yes, and the military too, if they have to. As in the past, workers need to remember that there are far more of us than there are police. Organize a strategy of resistance. As for the military, that's full-blown class war. If you see the military on the streets, then it's a sign of a fascist state. As in the past, remind the soldiers (and police) that they are our brothers and sisters and ask them to join us, the people that they should be protecting rather than the plutocrats. Then you fight back against those who continue to attack us, with equal force.

Given the globalization of the production process, you cannot have islands of socialism like western Europe in a capitalist world. Such nations will ultimately be outcompeted by the lowest-cost production regions. To stop the race to the bottom we must first change the power structure within the current global hegemon and then push for reforms of international capitalist institutions like the WTO. For the American working class to achieve equality, workers must develop class consciousness which can be transformed into solidarity. This implies moving from becoming aware of one's class position to becoming willing to act on it in solidarity with others. Unions must stop expending limited resources on strategies that are bankrupt, such as political contributions. For example, the Republican and Democratic parties from Clinton to Bush to Obama have passed free trade agreements with virtually no labor (or environmental) protections, despite labor's intense lobbying. Instead, our funds must be used for organizing, combined with worker education to raise class consciousness.

Workers have more power than they realize beyond withholding their labor power, which is what the old labor movement did through general strikes. As a class, workers can also withhold their political participation in an inherently biased political system, denying it the illusion of legitimacy. This is what the civil rights leaders did when they refused to conform to segregationist laws through civil disobedience. Workers also have a third power: to withhold their economic participation in biased economic structures. This can be done through the new radical forms of resistance outlined here. To be successful the working class must realize that all these tools of resistance have been legislated out of existence by the elite because of their effectiveness. The Walmarts of the world will not provide living wages unless they see a fundamental threat to their private property and the bottom line.

If the working class engages in new radical action it can expect violent reactions from the elite. It is this violence that we must resist with counter-violence of our own to bring about fundamental change. Finally, even if such action does not result in the immediate attainment of our goals it at the very least stops the deterioration of our condition. This is a neglected point in the debates over the effectiveness of radical resistance: what would have been done had workers not shown their willingness to fight back? How much worse are things when power holders do not expect resistance to their policies? Obviously, these questions cannot be quantified, yet the point is real.

What should we fight for other than taking control of corporate boards? Some suggestions include, but are not limited to, demanding through direct action:

1. The supremacy of community decision making over corporate governance: direct political and economic democracy.
2. Free and equal public education at all levels and the nationalization of all private educational institutions.
3. Prohibition of corporate governance or involvement in news media and the creation of an independent public foundation with tax funds to finance free and independent journalism with a tenure system.
4. All laws providing full and equal treatment to all individuals and groups.
5. Sustainable development and the use of renewable resources for the protection of the environment.
6. Family planning and a woman's right to make her own reproductive decisions with the availability of the required services.
7. Zero-tolerance policies for conflicts of interests for government positions at all levels.
8. Zero political patronage positions at all levels of government.
9. Zero corporate involvement in the political process at all levels.
10. Elimination of corporate wealthfare.
11. Repeal of the fiction of corporations as legal persons to establish accountability.
12. Free, single-payer, universal, quality, comprehensive health care as a human right.
13. A guaranteed minimum living standard for all, including income and universal quality housing.

14. Fair trade and trade only with democratic regimes respectful of human rights.

These demands alone would revolutionize the labor movement.

Notes

1. Aronowitz, 2005; Davis 1986; Harrison and Bluestone, 1990; Mishel et al., 2003–2009.
2. Zepezauer, 2004.
3. U.S. Census Bureau, Historical Income Tables-Households.
4. U.S. Census Bureau, Historical Poverty Tables.
5. U.S. Department of Labor, Series Id: LNS14000000.
6. U.S. Census Bureau, Historical Income Tables-Households.
7. Lewis, 2004.
8. Piven and Cloward, 1971.
9. Fording, 1997.
10. Ibid.
11. Mills, 2001 [1948].
12. Adler 2000; Davis 1986.
13. Domhoff, 2010.
14. Flood, 1989/90; Lerner, 1996.
15. Thoreau, 1969 [1849].
16. Lerner, 1996.
17. Winner-take-all, first-past-the-post, or simple plurality is a voting system in US elections by which the winner of a political district is the person with the most votes. There is no requirement that the winner gain an absolute majority of votes. A political party that wins 20% of the vote in every district, but not the majority of votes, will wind up with no representatives in congress. A party with a simple majority vote in every district can theoretically control all seats in congress. In parliamentary systems, candidates receive seats based on proportional representation reflecting the proportion of votes received overall. Under such systems, a party receiving 20% of all votes will hold approximately 20% of the parliamentary seats.
18. Some have argued that the United States is a one-and-a-half political party system because the policies of the two major parties are practically indistinguishable from each other.
19. National Priorities Project.
20. Head Start Bureau.
21. Zepezauer, 2004.

22. Ibid.
23. Ibid.
24. Ibid.
25. Ibid.
26. Ibid.
27. Public Citizen, 2002.
28. Lewis and Allison, 2002. Figures are for 1996.
29. Palast, 2004.
30. Typically, socially necessary labor is the amount of labor required by a worker of average skill and productivity, working with tools of the average productive potential, required to produce a given commodity. However, from a "cost" perspective it can also refer to the amount of work time required for a worker to earn enough to "reproduce" their labor power, e.g., raise children.
31. Brecher, 1997; Cole, 1999; Graham and Gurr, 1969; Kerner Commission, 1968; Rossi, 1973.
32. Brecher, 1997.
33. Leicht and Fitzgerald, 2007.
34. Zepezauer, 2004.
35. Pleming, 2005.
36. Eckholm, 2005: A9.
37. Zepezauer, 2004.
38. Ibid.
39. On December 3, 2009, GE and US cable TV operator Comcast announced a buyout agreement for NBC Universal. When the sale completes, Comcast will own 51% and GE 49% of NBC Universal. GE will also buy out Vivendi's 20% minority stake in the company. Vivendi completed the initial transaction on September 27, 2010, selling a $2 billion stake to GE (approximately 7.66%). The remaining 12.34% of NBC Universal would be sold to GE, pending completion of a sale to Comcast. US regulators approved the proposed sale on January 18, 2011.
40. Ibid., p. 98.
41. National Retail Security Survey, 2002.
42. Ibid.
43. Domhoff, 1975; Domhoff, 2010; Palast, 2004.
44. Domhoff, 2010.
45. Ibid.
46. McLean and Elkind, 2003.
47. Ibid.
48. Ibid.

49. Ibid.
50. Ibid.
51. Ibid.
52. Creswell, 2005.
53. Wong, Grace. "Kozlowski gets up to 25 years." September 19, 2005. http://money.cnn.com/2005/09/19/news/newsmakers/kozlowski_sentence; Roberts, Joel. "Tyco Execs Found Guilty." June 17, 2005. http://www.cbsnews.com/stories/2005/06/17/national/main702747.shtml.
54. Crawford, Krysten. "Ebbers gets 25 years." September 23, 2005. http://money.cnn.com/2005/07/13/news/newsmakers/ebbers_sentence.
55. CNNMoney.com. "Adelphia founder sentenced to 15 years." June 20, 2005. http://money.cnn.com/2005/06/20/news/newsmakers/rigas_sentencing.
56. Latimes.com. "Citigroup in Pact on Global Crossing." March 3, 2005. http://articles.latimes.com/2005/mar/03/business/fi-global3.
57. BBC.com. "Buffett warns on investment 'time bomb.'" March 4, 2003. http://news.bbc.co.uk/2/hi/2817995.stm.
58. Morgenson and Van Natta, 2009.
59. Isidore, Chris. "Fed made $9 trillion in emergency overnight loans." December 1, 2010. http://money.cnn.com/2010/12/01/news/economy/fed_reserve_data_release/index.htm.
60. Allen 1977; Domhoff, 2010; Mariolis, 1975; Mintz and Schwartz, 1985; Mizruchi, 1992; U.S. Senate Committee on Governmental Affairs, 1978b.
61. Domhoff, 1975.
62. U.S. Senate Committee on Governmental Affairs, 1978a.
63. Domhoff, 1975.
64. Ross and Yinger, 2002; Rummel, 2004.
65. Starkman and Mayer, 2005.
66. During the 2006 midterm elections, political controversy emerged over voter registration fraud by four ACORN employees. In 2009, selectively edited videos were released by two conservative activists using a hidden camera to elicit damaging responses from low-level ACORN employees that appeared to advise them how to hide prostitution activities and avoid taxes. This created a nationwide controversy resulting in a loss of funding from government and private donors. On November 2, 2010, ACORN filed for Chapter 7 liquidation, effectively closing the organization.
67. Arditi, 2004: 13.
68. Ibid.
69. Ibid.
70. See, for example, Michael Albert and Robin Hahnel. *The Political Economy of Participatory Economics* (NJ: Princeton University Press, 1991). "Parecon," or participatory economics, is an economic system proposed by

Michael Albert and Robin Hahnel, among others. It uses participatory decision making as an economic mechanism to guide the production, consumption and allocation of resources in a given society. Proposed as an alternative to capitalist and centrally planned economies, it is described as "an anarchistic economic vision" under which the means of production are owned by the workers.
71. Adamic, 2008.

Conclusion:
A Call to *Action!*

"What country can preserve its liberties if its rulers are not warned from time to time that their people preserve the spirit of resistance? Let them take arms."

Thomas Jefferson

Politicians will not bring change, they are corrupted products of the system that produced and financed them. The only difference among them is the degree of sympathy and remorse. Some may be sympathetic to the working class while they themselves continue to serve as corporate vassals. Fewer yet may express remorse for the repeated rape of the working class that they facilitate. However, the majority of politicians come from the middle and upper classes and are thus by definition our class enemies with a fundamentally different zeitgeist let alone opposing class interests.

The mass media is no more than a tool for the elite to perpetuate legitimizing myths to preserve the status quo. The only other function of the mass media is marketing to generate consumption for basic and mostly imaginary needs to increase corporate profits. There is no objectivity in any media. Corporate media, however, lacks any independence, does not perform any type of journalism; it is simply an advanced propaganda tool. It controls what you see, how you see it, and the parameters of the public debate should there even be one.

Educational institutions in the Anglo-Saxon countries, especially the United States, have ceased to exist, at least in the traditional sense. They have been degraded into educational (often for-profit) corporations for the production of non-critical drones to staff the military-educational-political-industrial Leviathan. Any and all critical thought is swiftly repressed. The few remaining critical professors have been more or less purged or intimidated into silence. Of the radical faculty remaining, there are few willing to lose their jobs for freedom of speech and social justice, let alone die for it. How is it possible for so few of the tenured faculty, politicians, and journalists to openly advocate revolution? Thomas Jefferson stated:

> Governments are instituted among Men, deriving their just Powers from the Consent of the Governed, that whenever any Form of Government becomes destructive of these Ends, it is the Right of the People to alter or to abolish it, and to institute new Government, laying its Foundation on such Principles, and organizing its Powers in such Form, as to them shall seem most likely to effect their Safety and Happiness.[1]

> I hold it that a little rebellion, now and then, is a good thing, and as necessary in the political world as storms are in the physical. Unsuccessful rebellions, indeed, generally establish the encroachments on the rights of the people, which have produced them. An observation of this truth should render honest republican governors so mild in their punishment of rebellions, as not to discourage them too much. It is medicine necessary for the sound health of government.[2]

> Most codes extend their definitions of treason to acts not really against one's country. They do not distinguish between acts against the government, and acts against the oppressions of the government. The latter are virtues, yet have furnished more victims to the executioner than the former, because real treasons are rare; oppressions frequent. The unsuccessful strugglers against tyranny have been the chief martyrs of treason laws in all countries.[3]

Fight back! The system is not designed for the poor or the worker. Design your own system, your own society. Leave behind decaying, corrupt social structures. Become your own thinkers and leaders. Revolt means militant resistance and struggle. The state would like to convince us that the violence that it monopolizes is unacceptable for workers except in the military. False class consciousness delegitimizes working-class violence. Educate yourself and others. Join activist groups, resist in the streets. Aspire to a better life or usher in the next wage-slave generation.

Notes

1. Jefferson, 2009.
2. Ibid.
3. Ibid.

Bibliography

Abu-Jamal, Mumia. 2004. *We Want Freedom: A Life in the Black Panther Party*. Cambridge, MA: South End Press.

Adamic, Luis. 2008. *Dynamite: The Story of Class Violence in America*. Oakland, CA: AK Press.

Adler, William M. 2000. *Mollie's Job: A Story of Life and Work on the Global Assembly Line*. New York: Scribner.

Allen, Michael. 1977. "Economic Interest Groups and the Corporate Elite Structure." *Social Science Quarterly* 58: 597–615.

Altenbaugh, Richard J. 1990. *Education for Struggle: The American Labor Colleges of the 1920s and 1930s*. Philadelphia: Temple University Press.

Alter, Jonathan. 2006. *The Defining Moment: FDR's Hundred Days and the Triumph of Hope*. Simon & Schuster.

Althusser, Louis. 2001. *Lenin and Philosophy and Other Essays*. Monthly Review Press.

Arditi, Benjamin. 2004. "From Globalism to Globalization: The Politics of Resistance." *New Political Science* 26: 5–22.

Aronowitz, Stanley. 1992. *False Promises: The Shaping of American Working Class Consciousness*. Durham: Duke University Press.

———. 2005. *Just around the corner: The Paradox of the Jobless Recovery*. Philadelphia: Temple University Press.

Asimakopoulos, John. 2000. *Comparative Analysis of European and American Working Class Attainments: Equality, Living Standards, and Social Structures of Accumulation*. Ph.D. dissertation, City University of New York.

Attewell, Paul, and David E. Lavin. 2007. *Passing the Torch: Does Higher Education for the Disadvantaged Pay Off across the Generations?* Russell Sage Foundation Publications.

Banister, Judith. 2005. *Manufacturing Employment and Compensation in China*. http://www.bls.gov/fls/chinareport.pdf.

Bebchuk, Lucian, and Jesse Fried. 2006. *Pay without Performance: The Unfulfilled Promise of Executive Compensation*. Harvard University Press.

Black, Stephanie, producer/director. 2003. *Life and Debt* [Documentary]. New Yorker Video.

Boesel, David, and Peter H. Rossi, (eds.). 1971. *Cities under Siege: An Anatomy of the Ghetto Riots, 1964–1968*. New York: Basic Books.

Bongiorno, Marylou, producer/director. 2007. *Revolution '67* [Documentary]. Bongiorno Productions Inc.

Brecher, Jeremy. 1997. *Strike!* Cambridge, MA: South End Press.

Burton, John Alexander, and Christian E. Weller. 2005. *Supersize This: How CEO Pay Took Off while America's Middle Class Struggled*. Washington, DC: Center for American Progress.

Carmichael, Stokely. 1971. *Stokely Speaks: Black Power Back to Pan-Africanism*. New York: Vintage Books.

Carwardine, William H. 1994. *The Pullman Strike: The Classic First-hand Account of an Epoch-making Struggle in US Labor History*. Chicago: C. H. Kerr Publishing Company.

Chomsky, Noam. 1989. *Necessary Illusions: Thought Control in Democratic Societies*. Boston: South End Press.

———. 1994. *Manufacturing Consent: Noam Chomsky and the Media*. New York: Black Rose Books.

———. 2002. *Media Control: The Spectacular Achievements of Propaganda*. New York: Seven Stories Press.

Chomsky, Noam, and Barry Pateman, eds. 2005. *Chomsky on Anarchism*. Oakland, CA: AK Press.

Churchill, Ward, and Jim Vander Wall. 2002. *The COINTELPRO papers: Documents from the FBI's Secret Wars against Dissent in the United States*. Cambridge, MA: South End Press.

Clawson, Dan. 2003. *The Next Upsurge: Labor and the New Social Movements*. Ithaca: ILR Press.

Cole, Michael D. 1999. *The L.A. Riots: Rage in the City of Angels*. Springfield, NJ: Enslow Publishers.

Conkey, Christopher. 2006. "Home-Equity Loans Level Off." *Wall Street Journal*, March 11, A6.

Cox, Robert W. 1987. *Production, Power, and World Order: Social Forces and the Making of History*. New York: Columbia University Press.

Creswell, Julie. 2005. "J.P. Morgan and Toronto-Dominion Agree to Settle Suits in Enron Fraud." *New York Times*, August 17, C3.

Dacus, Joseph A. 1969. *Annals of the Great Strikes in the United States: A Reliable History and Graphic Description of the Causes and Thrilling Events of the Labor Strikes and Riots of 1877*. New York: B. Franklin.

Dahrendorf, Ralf. 1959. *Class and Class Conflict in Industrial Society*. Stanford, CA: Stanford University Press.

Davis, Mike. 1986. *Prisoners of the American Dream: Politics and Economy in the History of the U.S. Working Class.* London: Verso Books.
Domhoff, G. William. 1975. *The Bohemian Grove and Other Retreats: A Study in Ruling-Class Cohesiveness.* New York: Harper Torchbooks.
———. 2009. Wealth, Income, and Power. http://whorulesamerica.net/power/wealth.html.
———. 2010. *Who Rules America? Challenges to Corporate and Class Dominance.* Sixth edition. Boston: McGraw Hill.
Dorgan, Byron. 2006. *Take This Job and Ship It: How Corporate Greed and Brain-Dead Politics Are Selling Out America.* New York: Thomas Dunne Books.
Eckholm, Erik. 2005. "Army Contract Official Critical of Halliburton Pact Is Demoted." *New York Times*, August 29, A9.
Fine, Sidney A. 1969. *Sit-down: The General Motors Strike of 1936–1937.* Ann Arbor: University of Michigan Press.
Flood, Lawrence. G., (Ed.). 1989/90. "Symposium on Unions and Public Policy." *Policy Studies Journal* 18: 357–363.
Foner, Philip Sheldon. 2002. *The great labor uprising of 1877.* Pathfinder Press.
Fording, Richard C. 1997. "The Conditional Effect of Violence as a Political Tactic: Mass Insurgency, Welfare Generosity, and Electoral Context in the American States." *American Journal of Political Science* 41: 1–29.
Frank, André Gunder. 2006. "Meet Uncle Sam–Without Clothes–Parading Around China and the World." *Critical Sociology* 32, no. 1: 17–44.
Friedheim, Robert L. 1964. *The Seattle General Strike.* Seattle: University of Washington Press.
Garrow, David J. 1989. *The Walking City: The Montgomery Bus Boycott, 1955–1956 (*Martin Luther King, Jr. and the Civil Rights Movement, Vol. 7*).* Brooklyn, NY: Carlson Publications.
Giroux, A. Henry. 1988. *Teachers as Intellectuals: Toward a Critical Pedagogy of Learning.* London: Bergin & Garvey.
———. 2007. *The University in Chains: Confronting the Military-Industrial-Academic Complex.* Paradigm Publishers.
Glen, John M. 1996. *Highlander: No Ordinary School.* Knoxville: University of Tennessee Press.
Global Policy Forum. 2006. "Total Number of Regional Free Trade Agreements 1948–2002." http://www.globalpolicy.org/socecon/trade/tables/rta.

Goodman, Barak, and Rachel Dretzin, directors. 2005. *The Persuaders* [Documentary]. Burbank, CA: PBS Home Video.

Gordon, M. David, Richard Edwards, and Michael Reich. 1982. *Segmented Work, Divided Workers: The Historical Transformation of Labor in the United States*. Cambridge University Press: Cambridge.

Graham, Hugh Davis, and Ted Robert Gurr. 1969. *The History of Violence in America*. New York: Bantam Books.

Gramsci, Antonio. 1971. *Selections from the Prison Notebooks of Antonio Gramsci*. Edited and translated by Quintin Hoare and G. N. Smith. New York: International Publishers.

Greenwald, Robert, producer/director. 2004. *Outfoxed: Rupert Murdoch's War on Journalism*. New York: Disinformation Company.

Greenway, John. 1970. *American Folksongs of Protest*. New York: Octagon Books.

Guerin, Daniel. 1970. *Anarchism: From Theory to Practice*. Translated by Mary Klopper. New York: Monthly Review Press.

Harrison, Bennett, and Barry Bluestone. 1990. *The Great U-Turn: Corporate Restructuring and the Polarizing of America*. New York: Basic Books. Reprint edition.

Harvey, David. 2006. *Spaces of Global Capitalism: A Theory of Uneven Geographical Development*. London: Verso.

Head Start Bureau. 2005. http://www.acf.hhs.gov/programs/hsb/research/2005.htm.

Hill, Lance E. 2004. *The Deacons for Defense: Armed Resistance and the Civil Rights Movement*. Chapel Hill: University of North Carolina Press.

Hirsch, Susan E. 2003. *After the Strike: A Century of Labor Struggle at Pullman*. Urbana: University of Illinois Press.

International Monetary Fund. IMF Members' Quotas and Voting Power, and IMF Board of Governors. http://www.imf.org/external/np/sec/memdir/members.htm#1.

Jefferson, Thomas. 2009. *Thomas Jefferson on Politics & Government: Quotations from the Writings of Thomas Jefferson*. http://etext.virginia.edu/jefferson/quotations/index.html.

Kerner Commission. 1968. *Report of the National Advisory Commission on Civil Disorders*. Washington: U.S. Government Printing Office.

King, Martin Luther. 1991. "If the Negro Wins, Labor Wins." In J. M. Washington (ed.), *A Testament of Hope The Essential Writings and Speeches of Martin Luther King, Jr.*, 201–207. New York: HarperCollins.

King, Tracey, and Ellynne Bannon. April 2002. "At What Cost? The Price That Working Students Pay for a College Education. Washington, DC: State PIRGs' Higher Education Project.
Klarman, Michael J. 2004. *From Jim Crow to Civil Rights: The Supreme Court and the Struggle for Racial Equality.* New York: Oxford University Press.
Kotz, M. David. 2006. "Contradictions of Economic Growth in the Neoliberal Era: Accumulation and Crisis in the Contemporary U.S. Economy." Paper presented at a session sponsored by the Union for Radical Political Economics at the Allied Social Sciences Associations Convention, Boston, January 8, 2006.
Kotz, M. David, Terrence McDonough, and Michael Reich, (eds.). 1994. *Social Structures of Accumulation.* Cambridge University Press: Cambridge.
Kozol, Jonathan. 1992. *Savage Inequalities: Children in America's Schools.* New York: Harper Perennial. Reprint edition.
———. 2005. *The Shame of the Nation: The Restoration of Apartheid Schooling in America.* New York: Crown Publishers.
Krajnc, Anita. 2000. "Popular Environmental Education: Lessons from the Labor and Civil Rights Movements." *New Political Science* 22: 341–360.
Krause, Paul. 1992. *The Battle for Homestead, 1880–1892: Politics, Culture, and Steel.* Pittsburgh, PA: University of Pittsburgh Press.
Kropotkin, Peter. 2005 [1892]. *The Conquest of Bread and Other Writings.* Edited by Marshall S. Shatz. Cambridge University Press.
Leicht, T. Kevin, and Scott T. Fitzgerald. 2007. *Post Industrial Peasants: The Illusion of Middle-Class Prosperity.* New York: Worth Publishers.
Lerner, Stephen. 1996. "Reviving Unions." *Boston Review* 21: 3–8.
Lewis, Charles, Bill Allison, and the Center for Public Integrity. 2002. *The Cheating of America: How Tax Avoidance & Evasion by the Super Rich Are Costing the Country Billions, & What You Can Do About It.* New York: HarperCollins.
Lewis, Diane E. 2004. "Worries about NLRB fuel union campaign." *The Boston Globe.* September 6.
Linder, Walter. 1963. *The Great Flint Sit-down Strike Against G.M., 1936–37: How Industrial Unionism was Won.* Bay Area Radical Education Project.
Lindsey, Almont. 1994. *The Pullman Strike: The Story of a Unique Experiment and of a Great Labor Upheaval.* Chicago: University of Chicago Press.

London, Steven. H. 1989/90. "The New Industrial Relations Ideology and the Decline of Labor." *Policy Studies Journal* 18: 481–493.

Macrine, Sheila, Peter McLaren, and David Hill. 2009. *Revolutionizing Pedagogy: Education for Social Justice Within and Beyond Global Neo-Liberalism*. Palgrave Macmillan.

Madigan, Tim. 2001. *The Burning: Massacre, Destruction, and the Tulsa Race Riot of 1921*. New York: St. Martin's Press.

Malcolm X. 1965. "The Ballot or the Bullet." In G. Breitman (ed.), *Malcolm X Speaks*: 23–44. New York: Grove Weidenfeld.

Mariolis, Peter. 1975. "Interlocking Directorates and the Control of Corporations: The Theory of Bank Control." *Social Science Quarterly* 56: 425–439.

Marx, Karl. 1973 [1858]. *Grundrisse*. New York: Vintage Books.

———. 1978a [1867]. *Capital, Volume One*. In Robert C. Tucker (ed.), *The Marx-Engels Reader*, pp. 294–438. New York: W. W. Norton.

———. 1978b [1862-63]. "Theories of Surplus Value." In Robert C. Tucker (ed.), *The Marx-Engels Reader*, 443–65. New York: W. W. Norton.

———. 1978c. *The Marx-Engels Reader*. Robert C. Tucker (ed.). New York: W. W. Norton.

Marx, Karl, and Frederick Engels. 1978 [1848]. "Manifesto of the Communist Party." In Robert C. Tucker (ed.), *The Marx-Engels Reader*, 469–500. New York: W. W. Norton.

McDonough, Terrence. 1994. "Social Structures of Accumulation, Contingent History, and Stages of Capitalism." In David M. Kotz, Terrence McDonough, and Michael Reich (eds.), *Social Structures of Accumulation*, 72–84. Cambridge: Cambridge University Press.

McLaren, Peter, and Peter Leonard (eds.). 1992. *Paulo Freire: A Critical Encounter*. New York: Routledge.

McLaren, Peter, Steven Best, and Anthony Nocella (eds.). 2009. *Academic Repression: Reflections from the Academic Industrial Complex*. Oakland, CA: AK Press.

McLaren, Peter, and Nathalia Jaramilo. 2009. *Pedagogy and Praxis in the Age of Empire: Towards a New Humanism*. Sense Publishers.

McLaren, Peter. 2005. *Che Guevara, Paulo Freire, and the Pedagogy of Revolution*. Rowman & Littlefield Publishers.

McLean, Bethany, and Peter Elkind. 2003. *Smartest Guys in the Room: The Amazing Rise and Scandalous Fall of Enron*. New York: Portfolio.

McMichael, Philip. 2008. *Development and Social Change*. Thousand Oaks: Pine Forge Press.

Meier, August, and Elliott Rudwick. 1975. *CORE: A Study in the Civil Rights Movement, 1942–1968*. Urbana: University of Illinois Press.
Mills, Wright C. 2000 [1956]. *The Power Elite*. Oxford University Press.
———. 2001 [1948]. *The New Men of Power, America's Labor Leaders*. Urbana: University of Illinois Press.
Mintz, A. Beth, and Michael Schwartz. 1985. *The Power Structure of American Business*. Chicago: University of Chicago Press.
Mishel, Lawrence, Jared Bernstein, and Boushey Heather. 2003–2009. *The State of Working America*. Cornell University Press.
Mizruchi, Mark S. 1992. *The Structure of Corporate Political Action: Interfirm Relations and Their Consequences*. Cambridge, MA: Harvard University Press.
Montgomery, David. 1976. "Labor in the Industrial Era." In Richard B. Morris (ed.), *The U.S. Department of Labor Bicentennial History of The American Worker*, 104–144. Washington, DC: US Government Printing Office.
Moody, Kim. 1997. *Workers in a Lean World*. London: Verso.
Morgan, Wayne Howard. 1973. *Eugene V. Debs: Socialist for President*. Westport, CT: Greenwood Press.
Morgenson, Gretchen, and Don Van Natta Jr. 2009. "Paulson's Calls to Goldman Tested Ethics." *New York Times*, August 8.
Morris, Aldon D. 1984. *The Origins of the Civil Rights Movement: Black Communities Organizing for Change*. New York: Free Press.
National Labor Committee. Various reports, 2000–2006. http://www.nlcnet.org/reports.
National Priorities Project, http://costofwar.com.
National Retail Security Survey. 2002. Center for Studies in Criminology and Law, University of Florida.
Ogbar, Jeffrey Ogbonna Green. 2004. *Black Power: Radical Politics and African American Identity*. Baltimore: Johns Hopkins University Press.
Organisation for Economic Co-operation and Development (OECD). 2005. *International Investment Perspectives*. OECD Publishing.
O'Hara, Phillip Anthony. 2001. "Recent Changes to the IMF, WTO and FSP: An Emerging Global Monetary-Trade-Production Social Structure of Accumulation for Long Wave Upswing?" Paper presented at the conference of the Association for Social Economics, New Orleans, January 5, 2001.
———. 2004. "A New Transnational Corporate Social Structure of Accumulation for Long-Wave Upswing in the World Economy?" *Review of Radical Political Economics* 36, no. 3: 328–35.

Palast, Greg. 2004. *The Best Democracy Money Can Buy*. New York: Plume.
Panitch, Leo, and Sam Gindin. 2005. "Finance and American Empire." In Leo Panitch and Colin Leys (eds.), *The Empire Reloaded: Socialist Register 2005*, 46–81. New York: Monthly Review Press.
Park, Mi. 2007. "South Korean Trade Union Movement at the Crossroads: A Critique of 'Social Movement' Unionism." *Critical Sociology* 33, no. 1–2: 311–44.
Peck, Jamie. 2002. "Labor, Zapped/growth, Restored? Three Moments of Neoliberal Restructuring in the American Labor Market." *Journal of Economic Geography* 2, no. 2: 179–220.
Peniel, Joseph E (ed.). 2006. *The Black Power Movement: Rethinking the Civil Rights-Black Power Era*. New York: Routledge.
Perlman, Selig. 1939. "Labor and Capitalism in the U.S.A." In A. Hilary (ed.), *Organized Labor in Four Continents*, 321–404. New York: Longman's, Green and Co.
———. 1966. *The Theory of the Labor Movement*. Harvard University Press.
Piven, Frances Fox, and Richard A. Cloward. 1971. *Regulating the Poor: The Functions of Public Welfare*. New York: Pantheon Books.
Pleming, Sue. 2005. "Halliburton's Iraq Deals Described as Contract Abuse." *Reuters*. June 27. http://www.alertnet.org.
Polanyi, Karl. 2001 [1944]. *The Great Transformation*. Beacon Press: Boston.
Proudhon, Pierre-Joseph. 1980 [1863]. *Principle of Federation*. Translated by R. Vernon. University of Toronto Press.
Public Citizen. 2002. "Corporate Fraud and Abuse Taxes Cost the Public Billions." http://www.citizen.org/documents/corporateabusetax.pdf.
Rocker, Rudolf. 1938. *Anarcho-Syndicalism*. London: Secker and Warburg.
Roediger, David. R., and Philip S. Foner. 1989. *Our Own Time: A History of American Labor and the Working Day*. Greenwood Press.
Rogers, Joel, and Streeck Wolfgang. 1994. "Workplace Representation Overseas: The Works Councils Story." In Richard B. Freeman (ed.), *Working under Different Rules*, 97–156. New York: Rusell Sage Foundation.
Ross, Stephen L. and John Yinger. 2002. *The Color of Credit: Mortgage Discrimination, Research Methodology, and Fair-Lending Enforcement*. Massachusetts Institute of Technology.
Rossi, Peter Henry (ed.). 1973. *Ghetto Revolts*. New Brunswick, NJ: Transaction Books.

Rummel, David, producer/director). 2004. *Secret History of the Credit Card* [Documentary]. United States: Frontline WGBH Educational Foundation.

Scott, E. Robert. 2007. *Costly Trade with China: Millions of U.S. Jobs Displaced with Net Job Loss in Every State.* Washington, DC: Economic Policy Institute.

Scott, E. Robert, Carlos Salas, and Bruce Campbell. 2006. *Revisiting NAFTA: Still Not Working for North America's Workers.* Washington, DC: Economic Policy Institute.

Shore, Elliott. 1992. *Talkin' Socialism: J. A. Wayland and the Radical Press.* Lawrence: University Press of Kansas.

Silver, Beverly. 2003. *Forces of Labor: Workers' Movements and Globalization Since 1870.* Cambridge: Cambridge University Press.

Smethurst, James. 2005. *The Black Arts Movement: Literary Nationalism in the 1960s and 1970s.* Chapel Hill: University of North Carolina Press.

Starkman, Dean, and Caroline E. Mayer. 2005. "Credit Card Consolidation: Bank of America to Buy MBNA." *Washington Post.* July 1, A1.

Stoper, Emily. 1989. *The Student Nonviolent Coordinating Committee: The Growth of Radicalism in a Civil Rights Organization.* Brooklyn, NY: Carlson.

Stowell, David O. 1999. *Streets, Railroads, and the Great Strike of 1877.* Chicago: University of Chicago Press.

Strain, Christopher. 2005. *Pure Fire: Armed Self-Defense as Activism in the Civil Rights Era.* Athens: University of Georgia Press.

Teitelbaum, Kenneth. 1993. *Schooling for "Good Rebels": Socialist Education for Children in the United States, 1900–1920.* Philadelphia: Temple University Press.

Theoharis, Jeanne. 2006. "'Alabama on Avalon' Rethinking the Watts Uprising and the Character of Black Protest in Los Angeles." In Peniel E. Joseph (ed.), *The Black Power Movement: Rethinking the Civil Rights-Black Power Era,* 27–53. New York: Routledge.

Thoreau, Henry David. 1969 [1849]. *Civil Disobedience [Resistance to Civil Government].* Boston: D. R. Godine.

Tuttle, William M. 1996. *Race Riot: Chicago in the Red Summer of 1919.* Urbana: University of Illinois Press.

Tyson, Timothy B. 1999. *Radio Free Dixie: Robert F. Williams & the Roots of Black Power.* Chapel Hill: University of North Carolina Press.

Umoja, Akinyele O. 2002. "We Will Shoot Back: The Natchez Model and Paramilitary Organization in the Mississippi Freedom Movement." *Journal of Black Studies*, 32: 271–294.

US Census Bureau. Foreign Trade Statistics, Foreign Trade in Goods (Imports, Exports and Trade Balance) with China. http://www.census.gov/foreign-trade/balance/c5700.html.

———. Historical Income Tables-Households. Table H-4. Gini Ratios for Households, by Race and Hispanic Origin of Householder: 1967 to 2007. http://www.census.gov/hhes/www/income/histinc/h04.html.

———. Historical Income Tables-Households. Table H-2. Share of Aggregate Income Received by Each Fifth and Top 5 Percent of Households All Races: 1967 to 2008. http://www.census.gov/hhes/www/income/data/historical/inequality/h02AR.xls.

———. Historical Poverty Tables. Table 4. Poverty Status of Families, by Type of Family, Presence of Related Children, Race, and Hispanic Origin: 1959 to 2008. http://www.census.gov/hhes/www/poverty/histpov/famindex.html.

US Department of Labor, Bureau of Labor Statistics, Division of International Labor Comparisons. 2009. "International comparisons of GDP per capita and per employed person 17 countries, 1960–2008." http://www.bls.gov/ILC.

———. Series Id: LNS14000000. Unemployment Rate. http://data.bls.gov/PDQ/servlet/SurveyOutputServlet.

———. Table 2. "Hourly compensation costs in U.S. dollars for production workers in manufacturing, 32 countries or areas and selected economic groups, selected years, 1975–2004." http://www.bls.gov/news.release/ichcc.t02.htm.

US Senate Committee on Governmental Affairs. 1978a. *Voting Rights in Major Corporations*. Washington, DC: US Government Printing Office.

———. 1978b. *Interlocking Directorates among the Major U.S. Corporations*. Washington, DC: US Government Printing Office.

Ward, Colin. 1982. *Anarchy in Action*. London: Freedom Press.

Weber, Max. 1978 [1922]. *Economy and Society: An Outline of Interpretive Sociology*. Edited by Guenther Roth and Claus Wittich. Berkeley: University of California Press.

Weinstein, James. 1984. *The decline of socialism in America, 1912–1925*. New Brunswick, NJ: Rutgers University Press.

Bibliography

Wendt, Simon. 2006. "The Roots of Black Power? Armed Resistance and the Radicalization of the Civil Rights Movement." In Peniel E. Joseph (ed.), *The Black Power Movement: Rethinking the Civil Rights-Black Power Era*, 145–165. New York: Routledge.

Wikipedia. "Anarchist Communism;" "Libertarian Socialism." http://en.wikipedia.org/wiki/Anarcho-communism; http://en.wikipedia.org/wiki/Libertarian_socialism

Wolff, Edward N. 2007. *Recent Trends in Household Wealth in the United States: Rising Debt and the Middle-Class Squeeze.* The Levy Economics Institute of Bard College and Department of Economics, New York University. http://www.levyinstitute.org/pubs/wp_502.pdf.

Wolff, Leon. 1965. *Lockout: The Story of the Homestead Strike of 1892: A Study of Violence, Unionism, and the Carnegie Steel Empire.* New York: Harper & Row.

Wolfson, H. Martin. 2003. "Neoliberalism and the Social Structure of Accumulation." *Review of Radical Political Economics*, 35, no. 3: 255–262.

World Bank. "Voting Powers." http://go.worldbank.org/GC8OQ79ES0.

Young, Marguerite. 1999. *Harp Song for a Radical: The Life and Times of Eugene Victor Debs.* New York: A.A. Knopf.

Young, Rick, producer/director). Air date: May 16, 2006. *Can You Afford to Retire?* PBS: Frontline.

Zaniello, Tom. 2003. *Working Stiffs, Union Maids, Reds, and Riffraff: An Expanded Guide to films about Labor.* Ithaca, NY: ILR Press.

Zepezauer, Mark. 2004. *Take the Rich off Welfare.* Cambridge, MA: South End Press.

Zinn, Howard. 2002. *SNCC: The New Abolitionists.* Cambridge, MA: South End Press.

Index

A

ACORN, 120–21, 128n66
Adamson Act, 84–85
Adelphia, 118
Afghanistan, xii, 112
African American media, 94
African Americans, iv–v; in labor movement, 78. *See also* Black Arts Movement; Black Power; civil rights movement
alternative media. *See* independent media
American Federation of Labor (AFL), 84
American International Group (AIG), 119
anarchism, 43, 44, 52
anarchists: Greece, 114; repression against, 77, 84
anarcho-syndicalism and anarcho-syndicalists, 57, 83
apparel industry, 18. *See also* shoe industry
Archer Daniels Midland, 116
Aristide, Jean-Bertrand, ix
Aristotle, 62
Arthur, Chester, 82
Arthur Andersen, 112, 118
arts, 76–77, 94, 94
Asimakopoulos, John, 123
Assange, Julian, xv, 121

B

Bakunin, Mikhail, 52, 54, 75
Bangladesh, 18
bankruptcy, 117, 120, 128n66
banks and banking, 39, 63–64, 113, 117–20. *See also* World Bank
Baraka, Amiri, 93
Best, Steve, 122–23
Black Arts Movement (BAM), 93, 94
Black Panther Party, 88, 97
Black Power, 87–88, 94–97

blacks. *See* African Americans
black studies, 93
Blankfein, Lloyd, 119
Blaze (blog), vii
Bloomberg, Mike, 40
Blum, Bill, xv–xvi
Bourdieu, Pierre, i
Brazil, 18, 20, 27
"Brazilification," 28
Bretton Woods agreement, 11, 17, 33n21
Britain. *See* UK
broker-dealers, 68n16
Bryn Mawr Summer School of Women Workers, xx–xxi
Buffett, Warren, 118–19
Bush, George W., xvii, 40, 113
business unionism, 103n3, 110
buyouts. *See* corporate buyouts

C

California energy crisis (2001), 118
California Proposition 14. *See* Proposition 14 (California)
Canada, 14
Carmichael, Stokely, 89, 95
cartels, drug. *See* drug cartels
censorship, 55
Central America, xi–xii
CEO pay. *See* executive pay
Chavez, Hugo, viii
Cheney, Dick, 40, 117
Chicago, 79, 80, 82, 83–84. *See also* Haymarket affair
China, 12, 13, 14, 18, 19, 28, 42, 55; FDI and, 20
Chomsky, Noam, 38–39, 41–42
CIA, xvi
CitiGroup, 118, 120
City University of New York, 42
civil disobedience, 74, 89, 110–12, 117. *See also* electronic civil disobedience; tax resistance
Civil Rights Act of 1964, 90
civil rights movement, 74, 86–102; timelines, 92

class consciousness, 50, 52, 66, 67n7, 70n53, 76, 77, 110; civil rights movement and, 88, 97; strikes and, 78
class struggle, 48, 75, 94
Clinton, Bill, 40
Clinton, Hillary, ix
clothing industry. *See* apparel industry
Coal Wars. *See* West Virginia Coal Wars
COINTELPRO, 89, 97, 98, 105n76
Cold War, x
colleges. *See* universities
college teachers. *See* university teachers
Comcast, 127n39
community work, 64
conflict of interest, 117
Congress of Racial Equality (CORE), 90, 92, 96, 105n76
conquistadores, v
consumer debt, 23–24, 59
consumption, 23–25, 60–63
Contras, xi
corporate boards, 39, 56–57, 67n8, 119
corporate buyouts, 127n39
corporate executives. *See* executives
corporate fraud, 117–18
corporate looting, 114–17
corporate offshoring. *See* offshoring
corporate personhood, 29, 125
corporate power, 39–41, 56, 58
corporate profits, 21, 112–13
corporate responsibility, 58
corporate subsidies, 115, 116
corporate taxes, 112–13, 116
cost, 62; benefit and, 70n82; of labor, 63
Coughlin, Charles, vii
"counter-hegemony" (term), 37n117
"counter ideology" (term), 37n115
credit, 64
credit card companies, 119, 120
credit card debt, 23–24
currency, 20, 33n21

Index

D

Deacons for Defense and Justice, 89, 95–96
death squads, xi
Debs, Eugene, 77, 80
debt, consumer. *See* consumer debt
Declaration of Morelia, xiv
defaulting on loans. *See* loan defaulting
demonization, 103n8
demonstrations and protests. *See* protests and demonstrations
depressions, 8, 27. *See also* Great Depression
derivatives (finance), 118
direct action, 44–45, 52, 66, 74, 109–10, 120–21, 125; civil rights movement and, 86–102; Greece, 114; labor movement and, 75–86. *See also* looting; strikes and strikers
Disney, 116
disposable personal income, 24
distribution, 60–61, 64, 71n89
dollarization, 20, 33n21
"dominant ideology" (term), 67n6
drama. *See* plays
drug cartels, xiii–xiv

E

Ebbers, Bernard, 118
economic panics, 8, 27
economic stagnation. *See* stagnation
economic stimulus policies. *See* stimulus policies
economics, trickle-down. *See* trickle-down economics
education, viii–ix, 41–42, 51–52, 55, 66, 75, 101–2, 130; civil rights movement and, 90, 92–94; inequality and, 61; K–12, vi; labor movement and, 76; TSI and, 123; of workers, xx–xxi. *See also* universities
Education Behind Bars, 123
Egypt, viii, xv, 122
eight-hour workday, 81–86
Einstein, Albert, 105
Eldredge, John, xiii–xiv
elections, 126n17
electronic civil disobedience, 121–22

Electronic Disturbance Theater, 121
Ellsberg, Daniel, xv
employee theft, 117
energy crisis, California (2001). *See* California energy crisis (2001)
Enron, 117–18
ethnic studies, vi
European Union (EU), 23
evolutionary social change, 52–55, 65–66
executions, 77, 101
executives: fraud by, 117–18; in government positions, 117; pay of, 61–62
exploitation, rate of, 35n78
Export Processing Zones (EPZs), 16

F

Fair Labor Standards Act (1938), 86
fair trade, 17, 34n49, 126
La Familia Michoacana, xiii, xv
Fanmi Lavalas, ix
FBI, 89, 97, 98, 105n76
Federal Reserve, 7, 30n1, 118, 119
Federation of Organized Trades and Labor Unions (FOTLU), 82–83
financial crises, 8, 27; twenty-first century, 7–8, 24–25, 68n16, 115, 116, 119
financial panics. *See* economic panics
Flanagan, Tom, xv
Flint Sit-Down Strike of 1936–37, 78, 80
Focus on the Family, xiii
Ford, Henry, 84
Fordism, 34n67
foreign direct investment (FDI), 12, 14–15, 20
foreign trade, 13–16, 124. *See also* fair trade
Fox Broadcasting, 41
France: GDP, 22; revolution of 1848, 54; wages, 18; works councils in, 57, 58
Frank, André Gunder, 13, 28
fraud, corporate. *See* corporate fraud
fraud, voter registration. *See* voter registration fraud
free riders (economics), 58, 71n83
free trade agreements, 13–16, 124

Index

Freire, Paulo, xvii, 69n30
Fry, Marquette, 98, 100

G

General Agreement on Tariffs and Trade (GATT), 14, 20
General Electric (GE), 113, 116, 127n39
general strikes, 78, 79, 80, 81, 82
Germany: GDP, 22; wages, 18; works councils in, 57, 58
Giffords, Gabrielle, viii
Gindin, Sam, 11, 16–17
Gini ratio, 21, 34n66, 108
Giroux, Henry, xix, xx
Glassman, Carol, 99–100
Global Crossing, 118
global segmentation of labor, 16–22, 71n92
Goldman Sachs, 40, 119
Gompers, Samuel, 73, 84
government military spending. *See* military spending
government representation, proportional. *See* proportional representation
government repression. *See* repression
Gramsci, Antonio, 29, 42, 43, 52, 69n30, 70n52, 75, 77
Great Britain. *See* UK
Great Depression, 7, 85
Great Railroad Strike of 1877, 78, 79
Greece, 25, 114
Gross Domestic Product, 20, 22, 23
Guatemala, xi–xii, 18

H

haircuts (finance), 68n16
Haiti, ix
Halliburton, 116, 117
Hampton, Fred, 97
Hayden, Tom, 99
Hayes, Rutherford, 79
Haymarket affair, 77, 84
Head Start, 112
health care, vii, 112, 119, 125
Highlander Folk School, xxi, 76, 92–93

Hill, Joe, 101
Hill, Lance, 96
home equity loans, 24
home mortgage loans. *See* mortgages
Homestead Strike of 1892, 78, 79–80
Hoover, J. Edgar, 97
Huckabee, Mike, xv
Hudi, Peter, ii, iii

I

immigration laws, vi
income, disposable. *See* disposable personal income
income tax, 113
independent media, 76, 123
India, 18
Indonesia, 18
Industrial Workers of the World (IWW), 77, 84–85
inequality, iii, x, 21, 51, 61, 109, 113. *See also* Gini ratio
information warfare, 121–22
intellectuals, 42, 54, 69n30, 70n52
International Bank for Reconstruction and Development. *See* World Bank
International Monetary Fund (IMF), 7, 11, 12; establishment of, 33n21
International Trade Organization, 14
International Trade Union Confederation, 29
International Workers' Association, 82
Internet, 121–21
interracial labor solidarity, 78
Iraq war, 112, 117
Ireland, 25
IWW. *See* Industrial Workers of the World (IWW)

J

James, Sharpe, 98–99
Japan, 13, 15, 23; GDP, 22; wages, 18
Jefferson, Thomas, 74, 130, 131
Jeffries, Shavar, 102
Johnson, Lyndon, 95, 100
Jones, LeRoi. *See* Baraka, Amiri
J.P. Morgan Chase, 118, 120

Index

K

Kerner Commission, 100
Keynes, John Maynard, 8
King, Martin Luther, Jr., 89, 97–98, 100, 105n76
King, Peter, xv
Knights of Labor, 77, 78, 83
Kondratieff, Nikolai, 31n9, 47
Kozlowski, Dennis, 118
Kropotkin, Peter, 43

L

labeling, viii, 97, 103
labor, 61–64. *See also* global segmentation of labor; socially necessary labor
labor arts, 76–77
labor councils, 57
labor laws, 74, 84–85, 85–86, 110, 111
labor movement, 29, 73–86, 110, 111, 124; MLK and, 98. *See also* business unionism; Social Movement Unionism (SMU); unionization rates
labor rights, 18
Lay, Ken, 117
legislation, vii, 74, 90, 110–12, 115, 124. *See also* immigration laws; labor laws
Lehman Brothers, 119
libertarian socialism, 43–44, 52, 58–59, 65–66; banking and, 64
literature, 76. *See also* plays
loan defaulting, 120–21
loans, home equity. *See* home equity loans
loans, home mortgage. *See* mortgages
"long waves," 31n9, 47
looting, 98, 99, 100, 110, 114, 120. *See also* corporate looting
Los Angeles, 79, 80, 100. *See also* Watts uprising (1965)
Ludlow Massacre, 84

M

machines, 62–63
Malcolm X, 73, 90, 94–95, 96

martial law, 80, 124
Marx, Karl, 7, 38, 62; *Capital*, 1; class consciousness and, 67n7; on production, 31n5–6; surplus value and, 32n13
El Más Loco. *See* Moreno Gonzalez, Nazario
McDonnell Douglas, 116
media, 125, 130; corporate control, 40, 41–42, 101, 113, 127n39; labeling by, viii; labor movement and, 76; "public interest" and, 116. *See also* African American media; independent media; social media
Merrill Lynch, 118
Mexican American studies, vi
Mexico, xii–xiv, 14, 16, 121; FDI and, 20; wages, 18
Mexico-US border, v–vi
Michoacán, xiii–xiv
Microsoft, 113
military spending, 116
militias, 79, 83
minimum wage, 108
money. *See* currency
Montgomery, David, 78–79
Montgomery Improvement Association (MIA), 92, 100
Moreno Gonzalez, Nazario, xiii–xiv
mortgages, 7, 118, 120
Mubarak, Hosni, viii, xv

N

NAFTA. *See* North American Free Trade Agreement (NAFTA)
National Association for the Advancement of Colored People (NAACP), 96, 105n76
National Labor Relations Act (1935), 85
National Labor Relations Board (NLRB), 109, 110, 111
National Labor Union, 82
Nation of Islam, 94
NBC, 116
NBC Universal, 127n39
Newark, New Jersey, 83, 90, 93, 94, 99–100, 102
New Deal, 86
New Growth Theory, 26
New Orleans, 78–79
New York City, 82. *See also* City University of New York

Index

Nicaragua, xi
No Apology (Romney), vii
nonviolence, 94, 95, 96–97
Norris-LaGuardia Act, 85
North, Oliver, x
North American Free Trade Agreement (NAFTA), 12–14, 16, 17, 18, 20

O

Obama, Barack, vii, xiv, xv
offshoring, 112, 118
"organic intellectuals," 42, 69n30
outsourcing, 17, 19
overcharging, 116, 118

P

Painter, Nell Irvin, 87
Palin, Sarah, xv
panics, economic. *See* economic panics
Panitch, Leo, 11, 16–17
"participatory economics," 128–29n70
Paterson, New Jersey, 84
Paulson, Henry, 40, 119
pay. *See* executives: pay of; wages
periodicals, socialist. *See* socialist periodicals
personal loan defaulting. *See* loan defaulting
Pittsburgh, 80
plays, 76, 93
Pope Alexander VI, v
poverty, 108–9
prices, 60–61, 63, 64. *See also* overcharging; transfer pricing
prisoner education programs, 123
production, 9–10, 31n5–6, 32n15, 50–52
productivity, 35n83
propaganda, 41–42, 130
property, 31n10, 48, 50
proportional representation, 126
Proposition 14 (California), 100
protests and demonstrations, 82, 83–84, 90
Proudhon, Pierre-Joseph, 48, 52, 54, 55

public wealth, 49–50, 62–63
Pullman Strike of 1894, 78, 79, 80
Puma, 19

R

race revolts, 94, 98–100, 114; timelines, 91
racism in banking, 120
Railroad Strike of 1877. *See* Great Railroad Strike of 1877
Reagan, Ronald, x–xii
rebellion: Jefferson on, 131
redlining, 120
replacement workers. *See* strike breakers
representation, proportional. *See* proportional representation
repression, 77, 80, 84, 85, 86, 101, 131. *See also* COINTELPRO
Requerimiento, v
revolution, 52–55, 97, 122
Rigas, John, 118
Rigas, Timothy, 118
Rios Montt, Efrain, xi
riots, race. *See* race revolts
Rocker, Rudolf, 44, 45, 52, 55
Romney, Mitt, vii
Roosevelt, Franklin D., 85
Rusk, Jeremiah, 84

S

sabotage, 123–24
St. Louis, 79
Sanchez, Sonia, 93
San Francisco State University, 93
Say's Law, 22, 35n74
scandals, 117–18, 128n66
Seattle General Strike of 1919, 78, 79, 80, 81
Securities and Exchange Commission (SEC), 40, 68n16
segmentation of labor, global. *See* global segmentation of labor
self-management, 57, 65, 79
shoe industry, 19
shoplifting, 117
Smethurst, James, 89

Index

SNCC. *See* Student Nonviolent Coordinating Committee (SNCC)
social change, evolutionary. *See* evolutionary social change
socialist libertarianism. *See* libertarian socialism
Socialist Party, 77
socialist periodicals, 76
socially necessary labor, 63, 127n30
Social Movement Unionism (SMU), 29, 37n119
social media, 122
Social Security Act (1935), 86
social structures of accumulation (SSA), 8–9 , 10, 17, 22–23, 45–46
social wealth. *See* public wealth
solidarity, xviii, 75–81 passim, 89, 124; arts and, 76–77, 93; eight-hour day and, 81, 86
songs, 76–77, 93
South Africa, 27
Soviet Union, 42, 53
Spain, 25, 52, 60
stagnation, 45
Steiner, David M., xix
Steward, Ira, 81, 82
stimulus policies, 7–8, 25, 115
stock ownership, 59, 113
strike breakers, 101, 111, 123, 123
strikes and strikers, 77–86, 110, 111, 114, 123. *See also* general strikes; sympathy strikes
Student Nonviolent Coordinating Committee (SNCC), 90, 93, 95
subsidies, corporate. *See* corporate subsidies
surplus value, 32n13
Swartz, Mark, 118
sympathy strikes, 78, 123

T

TARP. *See* Troubled Asset Relief Program (TARP)
taxation, 111, 112–13, 115, 116
tax resistance, 112, 116
T-bills. *See* Treasury bills
Tea Party Movement, iv, vii
theater, 76, 93
theft. *See* employee theft; looting
Theoharris, Jeanne, 99

Theory in Action, 123
think tanks, 117, 122–23
three-hour workday, 63
trade, foreign. *See* foreign trade
trade agreements, 15. *See also* free trade agreements
trade deficits, 14, 20
transfer pricing, 113
Transformative Studies Institute (TSI), 122–23
treason, 131
Treasury bills, 13, 115
trickle-down economics, 22, 35n74
Troubled Asset Relief Program (TARP), 115, 119
Tunisia, 122
Tuscaloosa, Alabama, 89
Tyco, 118

U

UK, 14–15, 25; GDP, 22; wages, 18
unemployment, 109
union bashing, x
union busting, x, 117
unionization rates, 109
unions. *See* labor movement
United Defense League (UDL), 90, 100
United Kingdom. *See* UK
United Mine Workers, 78
universities, 42, 93; corporatization, 122; Venezuela, viii
university teachers, 122, 130–31
US-Mexico border. *See* Mexico-US border

V

value, 62. *See also* surplus value
Venezuela, viii–ix
Via Campesina, 29
vigilantism, viii
violence, xv–xvi, 94–95, 96, 109–10, 123, 125, 131. *See also* death squads
Vivendi, 127n39
Volver a Marx conference, xii–xiv

Index

voter registration, 92
voter registration fraud, 128n66
voting systems, 126n17

W

wages, 18, 21, 26, 60–64, 113. *See also* minimum wage
Wagner Act. *See* National Labor Relations Act (1935)
Walker, Scott, xii
wars: cost of, 112
Watts uprising (1965), 98, 99
wealth, 48–50; distribution of, 59. *See also* inequality; public wealth
"wealth effect," 36n89
"wealthfare," 111, 116. *See also* corporate subsidies
welfare, 116
welfare bashing, x–xi
West Virginia Coal Wars, 84
WikiLeaks, xiv–xv, 121
Wild at Heart (Eldredge), xiii–xiv
Williams, Robert F., 94, 96–97
Winnick, Gary, 118
Wisconsin, xii
Wobblies. *See* Industrial Workers of the World (IWW)
Women of Summer, xx
work. See labor
workday, eight-hour. *See* eight-hour workday
workday, three-hour. *See* three-hour workday
workers, replacement. *See* strike breakers
workers' movement. *See* labor movement
workers' power, 57, 58
workers' rights. *See* labor rights
worker theft. *See* employee theft
working-class culture, 76–77
working-class intellectuals. *See* "organic intellectuals"
works councils, 57–58
World Bank, 10–12; establishment of, 33n21
WorldCom, 113, 118
World Trade Organization (WTO), 7, 10, 17, 20, 124

X

X, Malcolm. *See* Malcolm X

Y

"yellow dog contracts," 85

About the Transformative Studies Institute (TSI)
www.transformativestudies.org

TSI is a fully volunteer social justice think tank managed and operated by a global team of scholar-activists, grassroots activists, and the concerned public. Our goal is to establish a tuition-free accredited graduate school to foster interdisciplinary research that will bridge theory with activism and encourage community involvement to alleviate social problems. TSI publishes independent peer-reviewed journals including *Theory in Action*, operates a speakers' bureau, fellowship program, and various community outreach projects, and provides consulting services and custom policy papers. TSI was created to provide an inclusive educational space for research and practice for social justice by academics, community organizers, activists, and political leaders.

About the Author

John Asimakopoulos is executive director of the scholar-activist Transformative Studies Institute (TSI) and works with a highly underprivileged student population at the Bronx campus of the City University of New York as an associate professor of sociology. His publications include articles and books focusing on the history of social movements and how they can inform a new global working-class movement for the ushering of epochal change toward a just society. His works champion the formation of a counter-ideology, independent working-class media and educational institutions, and direct action toward this end. John's interest in the working-class stems from his parents who obtained only third-grade educations. They worked as landless farmers in Greece and later as immigrant factory workers in the United States. Early on in life, John observed that his parents' hard work was never rewarded, pushing him to think of social justice. Ever since, he has dedicated his life to promoting equality and social justice for all people.

CPSIA information can be obtained at www.ICGtesting.com
264912BV00001B/4/P